STREETSMART
TELESELLING

The 33 Secrets

STREETSMART TELESELLING

The 33 Secrets

Jeff Slutsky
Marc Slutsky

Prentice Hall Englewood Cliffs, New Jersey

Library of Congress Cataloging-in-Publication Data

Slutsky, Jeff
    Streetsmart teleselling : the 33 secrets / by Jeff & Marc
Slutsky.
       p.   cm.
    Includes bibliographical references.
    ISBN 0-13-851858-0
    1. Telemarketing. 2. Telephone selling. I. Slutsky, Marc.
II. Title.
HF5415.1265.S58   1990
658.8′4—dc20   90-7037
                                            CIP

ISBN 0-13-851858-0

Printed in the United States of America
10 9 8 7 6 5 4 3 2

Business & Professional Division
PRENTICE HALL   Englewood Cliffs, New Jersey 07632

Foreword

Anyone who has recently taken a business trip to New York, Chicago, or San Francisco knows how outrageously expensive out-of-town selling is today. With sky-high prices for airfares, hotel rooms, taxis, and meals, there has to be a better way to conduct out-of-town business.

Interestingly, while the cost of doing business has skyrocketed during recent years, it actually costs less today to sell via telephone. With the splitting up of AT&T and the competitiveness injected into the long-distance industry by the entry of several new, innovative carriers, rates have actually gone down—an uncommon happening in today's business world with its spiraling costs. Putting aside the economic factor, tele-selling is still by far the most productive way to use your time. But you have to know how to do it right. For obvious reasons, selling on the telephone is different from an in-person call. Your shining smile, new suit, and slap-on-the-back joke telling do not come across quite the same way on the telephone as they do during an eyeball-to-eyeball sales presentation. Selling on the telephone takes a different set of techniques, and the vast majority of salespeople simply have not developed the proper skills to do it effectively.

So what do they do? Either they fumble their way through telephone sales presentations or they shy away from making them altogether. Fortunately, it doesn't have to be this way—there *is* a solution. The solution is to put in time and effort to learn how to sell on the telephone. Jeff and Marc Slutsky tell you how to do it the painless way. They offer 33 secrets, and each of these gems has been field tested and promises immediate results. You can read these secrets one by one, practice them, and, within a month, you'll have picked up enough tips to realize sizable increases in your sales production. You'll learn everything from getting past the gate-keeper to handling objections to closing sales. There's also an excellent chapter on servicing customers via the telephone, so you can improve customer satisfaction, generate repeat orders, and obtain referrals. Best of all, Jeff and Marc won't tell you to do anything that they haven't done personally. They're super salespeople and have earned the right to tell others how to sell via the telephone.

The wave of the future demands tele-selling, and those salespeople who resist will fall by the wayside. Although it's been more than a century since the telephone was invented, the phone has finally come into its own as the greatest sales tool ever—providing, of course, that you know how to use it! Let me share a secret of my own with you that Jeff and Marc forgot to put in the book: Secret Number 34 is that *StreetSmart Tele-Selling: The 33 Secrets* does work and can make an important difference in your selling career. But that's up to you!

Robert L. Shook

An Introduction to StreetSmart Tele-Selling

Now you can learn how to increase your sales while spending less time selling. *StreetSmart Tele-Selling: The 33 Secrets* can help you develop your own telephone selling program, geared for your specific product or service, so that you get the most out of your selling effort.

Our book offers proven ideas useful in all aspects of getting sales. You can gain important skills designed to help you cold call, qualify your leads, set up appointments, close the sale, and get the order using the phone—even follow up after the close. *StreetSmart Tele-Selling: The 33 Secrets* provides you an opportunity to master the techniques required to dramatically increase sales. At the same time, you can learn how to reduce the cost, both in time and money, of each sales call.

Use of telemarketing is growing dramatically. Many companies that previously had not considered using the telephone as a primary marketing tool are now taking a long, hard look at this powerful marketing resource. Regardless of the product or service —whether it is high ticket or low ticket—there are ways you can use telemarketing to streamline your sales efforts. According to an article in *High-Tech Marketing* magazine:

> International Data Corp. (Framingham, MA) collected marketing budget data from 402 high-technology marketers in 10 industries. The results are divided into: 1) advertising, 2) promotion/public relations, 3) direct marketing/telemarketing, 4) sales/distribution,

and 5) market research. Trends suggest that advertising expenditures are falling in response to the slump in the high-tech markets. Firms are advertising more selectively, balking at rate increases, and being choosey about trade show participation. However, some analysts predict that only companies *willing to spend for direct marketing and telemarketing will be successful competitors* in the face of rising costs.[1]

This is just one example of how telemarketing has the potential to make a positive impact on your sales efforts. The key to that impact lies in embracing telemarketing as a primary marketing medium. More important, however, is *using that medium properly so you get the results you want and need.*

You can start with the ideas and techniques we explain in this book. Then you must take the ideas and techniques one step further. You must practice them until they become second nature to you. You must do this on your own. No one can do it for you.

Many great selling and telemarketing books and audio tapes are available. A number of them have some very good ideas. Some are written by friends and associates of ours who have contributed techniques and ideas for this book, including: George Walther, author of *Phone Power* and *Effective Telemarketing;* Bill Bishop, author of *The Million Dollar Presentation* and *Prime Prospects Unlimited* (formerly *Gold Calling*); and Robert L. Shook, author of (among many) *Successful Telephone Sales in the 90s, The Perfect Sales Presentation,* and *Hard Ball Selling.*

Simply put, however, books and tapes alone are not enough. When you boil it down, there are three elements that can make a difference to sales and telemarketing campaigns: talent, determination, and training.

The first two—talent and determination—we assume you bring with you. After all, by reading this book you are showing your desire to improve and enhance your sales skills. You would not be this far in your sales career without some raw talent. But now comes the hard part: training. You need to refine your talent and channel your energies so that they help you become more effective and efficient as a telephone selling professional.

---

[1] Alicia Orr, "The Cost of Marketing," *High-Tech Marketing* 3, 9 (September 1986): 17–63.

You will find that the techniques and tips in *StreetSmart Tele-Selling: The 33 Secrets* can be adapted to work for many products and services: tangible or intangible, high ticket or low ticket. You will discover that our book is applicable on many levels, including local, regional, national, or even international sales. Thus, the book can help you get the most out of your sales efforts—and increase your commission checks!

Your first step, as we explain in Chapter 1, is to develop your own tele-selling strategy so that you have an effective approach. This step is of paramount importance in getting the results you want for selling your particular product or service. You must then learn how to get past the gatekeepers. As we describe in Chapter 2, these are the secretaries and assistants who cannot say yes but who can always say no. They are often referred to as buffers or filters, as well as gatekeepers, and they have the power to keep you from talking to the person who has the power to give you the sale. In some cases, the gatekeeper is a decision influencer who has to take your message to the decision maker for you. Chapter 2 shows you how to get the most out of this unique situation.

Once you get past the gatekeeper, you must know how to make your initial contact with your prospect. Chapter 3 focuses on this very important topic, because what you say in the first 10–20 seconds determines the success you will have with that particular customer.

Chapter 4 focuses on helping you get from prospective customers the time and attention you need to be effective. You learn how to qualify your lead and set up appointments by phone—even if you plan to close the sale on the phone. The techniques in this chapter enable you to spend your time only with those leads who are in a position to buy what you are selling.

Improving your telephone sales presentation is the focus of Chapter 5, and Chapter 6 explains some special skills you need to deal with procrastinators and to overcome objections from customers who keep postponing decision making. Such customers are, perhaps, the most frustrating and deadly for the professional telephone salesperson. We show you how to move them off dead center. You also learn how to avoid answering objection after objection and how to get your prospect away from an objection and back into a position to close the sale.

You may wish to use the phone only up to this point. Using the phone to make qualified appointments in and of itself makes the entire program worth your while. But just think for a moment. What if it were actually possible to get the order over the phone without making an in-person sales call. We are not just talking about selling circus tickets for a charity here. We are talking about insurance policies, cars, investments, real estate, advertising, and consulting services closed over the phone. Chapter 7 addresses an idea we call phone closing—something we find very exciting. Nothing in tele-sales is more rewarding than working by phone with a prospect for a period of time, then one day getting a contract and a check for many thousands of dollars delivered to your door.

Of course, it is much easier to get more money out of an existing customer than to bring in a new customer. So Chapter 8 explains how to service your customers over the phone. Chapter 9 tells you how to double your results. You will discover many ways to save even more time and money, and you will learn how to evaluate and improve your performance. The result is that you will be able to make more money in less time.

You have an exciting and ambitious undertaking ahead of you —one that has the potential of showing you how to increase your sales. Every technique and idea in this program has been proven in the field. There are no theories here. It is up to you to make them work for you. Now we are ready to launch into the exciting world of StreetSmart Tele-Selling.

Acknowledgments

The authors acknowledge the contributions of various friends, family, and associates who have enriched the pages of this book with their wisdom, advice, and support—among them: Bill Bishop, Michael Brennan (our favorite guinea pig), Jeff Herman (our favorite literary agent), Michael LeBoeuf, Dorothy Leeds, Mark Sanborn, George Walther (our favorite phone expert), and especially Tom Power, a very understanding and patient editor. A special thanks to Bob Shook, who made this effort possible. And a very special thanks to our baby brother, Howard Slutsky, who conducted a great deal of research for us and who, for his efforts, was compensated only with one Big Mac, fries, and a chocolate shake.

Contents

1

Developing a StreetSmart Tele-Selling Strategy

STREETSMART TELE-SELLING SECRET #1

To get the best results from your selling efforts, choose the most effective tele-selling strategy. This strategy should be based on the appropriate combination of tele-selling phone calls and mail follow-ups for your particular product or service.

Your first step toward increasing your sales is to develop an effective StreetSmart Tele-Selling strategy geared specifically to your product or service. You can use StreetSmart Tele-Selling to sell anything by phone—as long as the strategy you develop puts your client in a buying position. The strategy you develop should suggest both the number and content of phone calls you need to make before you are in a position to close the sale. You also need to consider the frequency and content of the follow-up mailers that you use to support your calling efforts.

The particular strategy you develop should also take into account many other aspects of the sale. These can include: (1) the type of product or service you sell, (2) the territory and customers you sell to, and (3) your own personal selling style. There is no right or wrong strategy, as long as the approach you use works for you. After all, the only thing that counts in selling is getting the sale and creating a base of happy customers who buy again and refer more business to you.

●

Building Up Nest Eggs. Mark works for a company that specializes in setting up retirement programs. He primarily sells life insurance policies but has a wide range of products available to help his clients achieve their financial goals. He started selling less than a year ago and found slow going on the road to success.

Then, one of his clients provided him with a list of leads. The client belonged to a professional organization, many of whose members would make excellent prospects for Mark's particular product offerings. With the help of his client, Mark sent out a letter on the client's letterhead, introducing Mark to the members of the organization. He then used the telephone to qualify the prospects and set up appointments with those prospects that had promise. As a result he got many qualified appointments that would otherwise have taken him many months to set up using the smile-and-dial cold call approach.

Overruling the Objection. Barbara had an entirely different situation. Her job was to sell the catering services of her company. She was starting from scratch; the company had never hired someone to sell before. She was left alone to develop her own selling strategy. She first targeted a few groups that her company had worked with before. One such group consisted of law firms that put on catered parties for their clients.

Barbara then used a local business publication to single out the top 25 law offices in the city. She got nowhere cold calling in person. Whenever she visited one of the law offices, she couldn't get through to anyone at all, let alone the right one. She also tried sending out letters to the offices, but this too was of no avail. Finally, with our help she put together a plan to call the offices first and talk to someone who was responsible for catering. She then qualified the prospects, sent some material as follow-up, and eventually met with them in person to work out a proposed menu.

This approach worked for her. Within just a few days, she got in to see the right people in some of the targeted law offices, and she eventually made some sales. Once Barbara started working with a few of the law firms, it became easier to get to make her presentations to some of the other law firms in the area. As a result, she was able to build a nice clientele.

Sewing Up the Loose Ends. One of the country's largest distributors of sewing machines had an entirely different problem. The firm had a well-developed sales force, but the bottom 10 percent of each sales rep's account list was not worth the time necessary to generate some action. These customers did not buy enough product to warrant visiting them in person, and, because they were not called on, they bought even less—a Catch-22 if you will. To help change that circumstance, we developed a telephone selling program in the corporate office. One telephone salesperson would work with all the sales representatives' bottom 10 percents that they were not working with anyway. The telephone salesperson's first goals were (1) to make sure the low-volume customers received some personal attention, even if it was by phone, and (2) to help them to increase their purchases. The next objective was to increase these customers' sales volume to a minimal level where it then made sense for the field sales representatives to work directly with them. In just a few short weeks, the telephone salesperson started getting sales from clients previously considered worthless.

With Strings Attached. John, one of the sewing machine company's more successful retailers, wanted a program that would help him during his slower season. He spent a lot of money on advertising, trying to get people in his front door. He knew that once they saw what he had to offer, there was a very good chance they would want to buy something. Unfortunately, the regular advertising was not pulling in as many customers as he wanted. So he tried a Tele-Selling approach.

Using a list of attendees from a sewing seminar he had sponsored earlier in the year, John made calls inviting them in to test out a brand new machine. He offered them a free gift just for coming in, trying out the machine, and answering some survey questions about it. With a single phone call he was able to get some of those people to come in for his offer, and he sold some of the upscale machines. His cost for this effort was far less than what he had spent on regular advertising.

Driving Me Away. A month after Jeff bought a new car, he needed some service work on it. The power antenna was broken because someone from the dealership had run his car through their automatic car wash with the antenna up. The dealership offered to fix it, but it never worked as it was supposed to. Jeff got tired of complaining and bringing his car in, so he just gave up. He vowed never to do business with the dealership again.

A few weeks later Jeff got a call from Sue, the dealership's customer service representative, asking how he liked his new car and the service he got. He told her that he loved the new car, but gave her an earful about the service and about the antenna incident. Within a few hours Sue called him back and said that the dealer would replace the antenna entirely at cost. She gave Jeff the figure and it sounded good to him, compared with what he would have had to pay to get it fixed on his own.

The antenna was fixed, and Jeff also had some other work done on the car. He was not totally satisfied but at least was brought from a definite negative to a more neutral feeling about the company. At least they had tried to rectify the dilemma. Jeff did not know if he would buy from them again, but as a result of their telephone effort to fix his problem, he decided he was more likely to give them a second chance.

The Sweet Smell of Success. One of the more creative and effective uses of telephone selling came to our attention when *Success Magazine* ran a small feature story about our Streetfighting tele-sales program, complete with a color photograph. As expected, we received a lot of phone calls, but one in particular was memorable. A man called and congratulated us on the article. He then explained that he has a company that takes such articles from magazines and creates attractive wood plaques. The article, the banner from the cover page of the magazine, and a personalized, engraved brass plate would create a handsome showpiece, and there was no obligation to keep it if we were not totally satisfied.

Because of the timeliness of his call, we ordered. We had seen similar things before and thought of doing them ourselves. We suspect that we could have had the same exact thing done for 50 percent less. Yet this person made the effort, and he no doubt has expanded his market base well outside of his hometown by using the phone. Now that's StreetSmart Tele-Selling!

As you can see, the phone can be used in a variety of situations as a primary, or even secondary, marketing tool. Each situation is different and requires its own unique approach. The key to succeeding is identifying your own objectives so that you can choose the appropriate telephone approach. By choosing a tele-selling strategy involving the most appropriate combination of telephone calls and mail follow-ups, you can sell almost any product or service over the phone. These strategies can range from a single phone call to a series of three or more phone calls combined with three or more mail follow-ups. We give a detailed explanation of each step in the process, so you can begin to understand which approach would be most effective for you.

The One-Call-Close Approach

The one-call-close approach is effective primarily for low-ticket items and products that are familiar to the buyer. Some typical applications of the one-call-close approach are charity fund raisers, long-distance services, and club membership drives. The one-call close can also be effective for add-on and follow-up sales in areas such as service contracts, renewals, or supplies. The reason this particular approach limits itself to familiar, low-cost products and services is because you get only one telephone call to make the sale. Usually this is not enough contact to give you the opportunity to build a good level of rapport with your customer. So the customer has to be familiar with what you are selling.

One element affecting your success with the one-call-close approach is the quality of the phone list. Soliciting support for a worthy cause using random calling from the phone book would yield far less response than working from a qualified list. You are likely to have greater response, for example, if you call supporters who have already donated to worthy causes as a result of a telephone solicitation. Or, if you can work from a list of people specifically interested in a particular charity or product, your success rate is likely to be much greater.

As a rule, the one-call close requires use of a script. There is often little flexibility in that script and, after just one or two objections from the called person, the telemarketer hangs up and tries the next number. For many telephone sales operations that use this approach, volume of calls seems to be more important than the quality of calls, and the callers get little, if any, training. They are simply instructed to smile and dial. With a large enough volume of calls, this approach can be very successful.

We used the one-call-close method as a training approach for new salespeople who would eventually employ more sophisticated approaches. For our necessary low-ticket item, we created a local public seminar on low-cost marketing. A small classified advertisement in the local paper promoted the seminar at $301 per seat. Once the ad ran, the new salespeople, working from a script, called targeted small businesses from the local yellow pages. For each call, the salesperson tried to get a commitment to attend the program. Passages in the script included: "This seminar has been advertised in the local newspaper for over $300 a seat, but if you act today, you can attend for half price."

We did not expect to make a lot of money on the seminar. The primary goal was to discover if a new salesperson had the talent to make sales over the phone. We knew from previous experience that a decent salesperson could put about 20 people in the program in three to four weeks.

Another reason we chose this route for training was so that any mistakes a new salesperson made would not jeopardize a possible major client. Trainees called only the "mom and pop" stores in town, with whom we would not normally have had an opportunity to work.

/According to an article in *Advertising Age* magazine, Texas Instruments was so successful with its telemarketing program that its Data Systems Group decided to telemarket computer maintenance contracts for two of TI's product lines. Telephone Marketing Services was paid an initial investment of less than $40,000 for 40–60 hours of creative design and setup. TMS then took the project in-house to save money. The Telephone Marketing Services staff called and sent letters to system owners with maintenance policies about to expire in two or three months. The telemarketers overcame the technical and educational challenges of dealing with very highly valued equipment. They also had to learn background information about Texas Instruments and the computer industry so they would be perceived by prospects as full-time company employees. The telemarketers provided callers with relevant information and closed deals on the phone as often as possible. The program was constantly modified as the telemarketers analyzed the material. They got through the secretarial screen to the decision maker by being logical, straightforward, and legitimate. TMS was recently selling renewal, parts, and service maintenance contracts for TI machines.[1]

Advertise-First/Phone Close Strategy

The advertise first/phone-close strategy usually works in two different ways. The most common way is by generating inbound inquiries—a sales method that is gaining popularity worldwide. According to an article in *Marketing* magazine, "Inbound telemarketing activity has nearly tripled, and trade sources predict an annual growth of 50 percent for the next five years."[2]

Incoming calls are usually generated by asking the reader, viewer, or listener to respond to an advertisement for more information. This can be done in several ways including:

1. a toll-free 800 number,
2. a prepaid business reply post card or envelope, and/or
3. as part of a research project or survey.

All these approaches can achieve the same goal: having a sales representative follow up. The main difference between this approach and most others is that the advertise-first strategy is *reactive*, while most other telephone selling strategies are *proactive*. That simply means that you are letting your advertising do your cold calling for you.

If your company provides leads by generating incoming calls through advertising, you have a real jump on other Tele-Sellers who have to cold call to dig up decent leads. To a degree, the leads you get from an advertising campaign are qualified. The degree to which they are qualified depends on the questions asked. The more you ask of a potential buyer in the advertising campaigns, the less total response you will get. However, the customers who do respond usually are more qualified.

---

[1]Nancy Zeldis, "Direct Marketing: In Telemarketing, Stay Straight, Simple," *Advertising Age* 58, no. 21 (May 18, 1987): s26–s27.

[2]Donna Dawson, "Direct Line to Sales Boom," *Marketing* (UK) (October 8, 1987): 45, 47.

Trade Journal

If your company is running an advertisement in a major trade journal and asks the reader to call a number for more information or a quote, you are likely to get more responses if the number is an 800 number. On the other hand, if the reader has to pay for the call you will get fewer responses, but the ones who do respond are probably much more interested in what you are selling, since they are paying for the call themselves. Depending on your product or service, either method can be effective. You should test to see which one yields the best results over time.

The other advantage to the advertising-first/phone-close approach is that in a cold-calling situation, your lead already has some exposure to your company and your product or service before you call. If the advertising was effective, it helps you at least to get in the front door. By the same token, however, if too much detailed information is given in the ad, the prospect may feel that he or she already knows enough about what you are selling to make a decision without you. This usually results in a more difficult sale, if you can make a sale at all.

Direct Mail

Of all the available forms of advertising, direct mail is the one medium that allows you to target the exact group you are going to call. A direct-mail campaign can be very effective, but its main disadvantage is its cost. You can spend a small fortune developing a direct-mail piece that you hope will not get tossed in the wastebasket at first glance. You then have to print it, fold it, and pay for a mailing list and postage. Also, direct mail is inefficient. Often, a three- to five-percent response is considered very good. In a later chapter, you will learn how to send a mailer that gets almost 100-percent readership.

If the company you work for provides leads or exposure obtained through advertising you at least know that the people you will talk to have expressed some interest in what you have to offer. But you still have to ask yourself one question: "Am I getting as many good, qualified leads as I want?" Most professional salespeople cannot get enough good qualified leads. Therefore, your telephone selling strategy should be one that enables you to get sales without depending on your company, vendor, or supplier to advertise for you. When they do advertise, it is a nice bonus, but you never want to become dependent for your commissions on what others may decide to do. The advertise-first phone close is an ideal approach, as long as your company or vendor is paying for the advertising. When the advertising costs come out of your own pocket, however, the technique can be costly. Of course, for every rule there is an exception. Although we usually suggest using the phone first before making calls, we recently received a very clever initial letter that helped the writer set up an appointment with us.

It was a letter, on letterhead, from the district manager of Automatic Data Processing. At the top of the letter, near the company's logo, a penny was taped to the paper. This got our attention. The letter said:

> Just One Penny . . .
>
> . . . . Is all you need to be in error on calculating your payroll taxes to experience a substantial penalty from the Internal Revenue Service.
>
> Automatic Data Processing can fully insulate your company from payroll tax penalties by paying and filing your payroll taxes for you.
>
> We assume full legal liability for the timeliness and accuracy of the payroll tax deposits, which means *NO* late charges or penalties *EVER.*
>
> I would like the opportunity to discuss the benefits of ADP's payroll/tax service and will call you in a few days to arrange an appointment.
>
> P.S. The penny is yours to keep . . . it is just one of many you will save by having ADP insulate you from tax penalties.

The letter's first sentence immediately illustrated the benefit in a clear and dramatic way. When the telephone call came a few days later, as promised in the letter, we made sure to take the call.

Publicity

Publicity can work for you in ways similar to the advertise-first/phone-close approach. When your company receives favorable news items, the publicity helps your prospects become more aware of your product or service. Another advantage of a favorable article or story is that, because it is not advertising, it has much more credibility with customers or clients. You will learn in Chapter 4 how to use this publicity to build credibility in your selling effort.

Trade Shows

Another version of the advertise-first/phone-close approach is using trade shows to generate leads for follow-up. This approach is very common and, if done properly, can be very cost effective. It also can be a disaster if not carefully planned out and executed. Here is an example of successful use of a trade show.

One of our clients was a health club that was the first in the market to feature Nautilus equipment. The client decided to participate in a trade show known as the "Sports, Vacation, and Boat Show," a very big event every year. Because the show promoter had never seen anything like Nautilus, he thought the equipment would be a big attraction to the show. He offered to provide the client three spaces for the price of one. He also agreed to place the client's booth near the center of the show, right by the area where the attractions took place.

The client moved a dozen pieces of Nautilus equipment to the show and negotiated free one-day passes for all members of the health club. Because the equipment was now at the Coliseum, members were invited to do their workout at the show. This worked out well because people were constantly on hand demonstrating the machines.

The salespeople's thrust was to get the passers-by who expressed interest in the health club to sign up for a free drawing. The entry form asked for name, address, phone, and a few other details. After the five-day show was done, each of the client's four sales reps was given an equal number of names. Using an outbound telephone selling approach, they called all the contestants and informed them that they had won a free introductory membership valued at $20. The sales reps did this on their own time. Some even made the calls from their homes. It was then their job to set up the appointments for the potential members' first visits.

The introductory membership entitled the potential members to three visits. It was the sales rep's objective to get the "winners" to the club and have them try out the complete line of Nautilus equipment. Once the prospects were at the club, the sales reps had a good close ratio, primarily because the program sold itself. They did not try to close anyone at the show. Doing so would have been inefficient because there were tens of thousands of potential buyers passing by. The key at the show was both to generate the lead and to loosely qualify it. Then the sales rep could follow up by phone after the show, when time was not at such a premium.

Yellow Pages

Many retail and local service businesses use advertisements in the Yellow Pages to generate inbound sales inquiries. The problem with Yellow Pages advertising is that it is very expensive. Plus, you have to contend with many directories that compete with the Yellow Pages: You have to decide which books to advertise in or you may feel the need to be in all of them.

Despite its high cost, for some types of businesses, Yellow Pages advertising can be a good vehicle for an advertisement-first/phone-close strategy. However, you should track the results you get from Yellow Pages advertising—and from any form of advertising for that matter. You need to get a good feel for how well such advertising is working for you. Then you should buy the smallest ad you feel will be effective without jeopardizing sales. Keep in mind, however, that Yellow Pages advertising is a tough thing to test, because new Yellow Pages come out once a year, and you have to make a twelve-month commitment.

Here is an important suggestion about the Yellow Pages: In your other advertisements, *do not* reference your Yellow Pages ad, particularly with text such as: "Look for our Yellow Pages advertisement." If your other advertising generates interest, why refer the potential customer to the one place that displays your ad together with all your competitors' ads. It makes it too easy for your customers to pick up the phone and do some comparison shopping.

Detecting an Opportunity to Double Business. Creative uses of Yellow Pages advertising have generated a great amount of inbound sales inquiries. After reading our first book, *Streetfighting,* a private detective in Akron, Ohio, was able to double his business with Yellow Pages advertising. One of his major competitors had an expensive half-page ad, while he had only a very small ad. Soon after the new Yellow Pages book came out, the competitor with the half-page ad went out of business. The StreetSmart private detective called the phone answering service that owned the phone number of the out-of-business competitor. For a little over $50 a month, the StreetSmart private eye was able to buy the service at that number. The move doubled his business almost immediately.

Getting Ripped Off. One of the more interesting examples of Yellow Pages advertising involves a small pizza chain in Denver that had to compete against Domino's Pizza. Domino's built its business on pizza delivery and recently was the second largest pizza chain in the United States. With such success, Domino's could afford a tremendous amount of advertising, including a very large ad in the Yellow Pages. The local chain could afford only a small one. Tough competition. When the new Yellow Pages book came out, the small chain ran an advertising campaign that allowed people to get two-for-one pizzas if they would bring in the Domino's Yellow Pages ad from the book!

Taking Toll

One very unusual variation of the advertise-first/phone-close approach was brought to our attention by Murray Raphel and Ray Considine, authors of *The Great Brain Robbery.*[3] A stockbroker on the East Coast had to pay a toll on his way to work every morning. Before he paid his toll, he would first look in his rear view mirror. If he saw a Lincoln, Cadillac, Porsche, Mercedes, or any car of that stature, he not only would pay his toll, he would pay the toll of the person behind him, as well, and leave his business card with the toll booth attendant. On the back of the card, he had printed: "If you think this is a creative and unique way of getting your attention, just think of what I can do for your portfolio. Call me so we can talk about it." He got more new clients from a 90-cent toll than from any other promotion or advertising he tried. It certainly was an effective and creative way of generating incoming sales calls.

Broadcast

Another example of an inbound or "reactive" telephone sales technique is a karate school that used a lot of television and newspaper advertising to generate leads. After an ad, there would be many phone calls. Most of the calls inquired about the price. It was the objective of the salespeople to set up a time when the prospects could come in and see the facilities. They knew that, in most cases, if they gave the price over the phone, they seldom got

---

[3]Murray Raphel and Ray Considine, *The Great Brain Robbery* (Self-published. Available from Murray Raphel Advertising, Gordon's Alley, Atlantic City, NJ 08401. 609/348-6646).

an opportunity to close. It was only after the prospect came to the school that the salespeople had an opportunity to get a sale. In this way, the karate school was using a hybrid strategy of the advertise-first approach and the strategy that follows, "one-call/appointment."

Telemarketing

Sometimes, telemarketing can be used as the "advertising" medium to generate new leads. Such was the case with Micom Systems (Semi Valley, CA), a maker of data communications equipment. Besides their telemarketing campaign, Micom Systems used an incentive program, called Fortune Hunter, that David Andrews & Associates had designed for them. It was a "proactive" program that not only offered rewards but also gave salespeople sales opportunities or leads. The Fortune Hunter program both increased sales in a down market and paid for itself. Distributors got additional sales leads every time they entered a claim for selling $15,000 worth of product. Nearly 2,000 leads throughout the United States were discovered, adding up to almost $2.2 million in potential new business. The contest was open to all distributor salespeople, sales managers, and anyone else directly involved in selling Micom products. A mystery caller awarded $50 to salespeople who recommended Micom and could answer questions that had been on training cassette tapes.[4]

One Call/Appointment Strategy

At the very least, every professional salesperson who makes cold calls in person should consider using the telephone for setting up qualified appointments. This is known as the one-call/appointment technique. By cold calling on the phone, instead of hitting the bricks and knocking on doors, you are able to handle a significant number of cold calls—perhaps four to five times as many leads in the same period of time. Then, if you really must visit a prospect in person, by calling first and setting up appointments, you spend time only with those prospects who are fully qualified to buy what you have.

[4] "Incentives—Distributors Fund a Fortune: How Micom Starts the Action," *Sales & Marketing Management* 136, no. 5 (April 1986): 104–105.

Your close ratio goes up dramatically and your motivation and enthusiasm go up as well.

Consider the following example of using the phone to set up an appointment: BI Rolatruc, a division of BI Industries of Sweden, is the United Kingdom sales and service subsidiary of one of the world's largest manufacturers of forklift trucks and automated handling. The company became increasingly dissatisfied with the growing expense of cold canvassing as a means of generating sales. As a result, BI Rolatruc decided to experiment with telephone marketing as a way to identify realistic prospects to pass along to the sales staff. The pilot program lasted only a few weeks, but results were encouraging. Potential customers responded favorably to the sales approach. Also, the company was able to determine the type of equipment the respondents used, as well as gather data on market awareness of BI Rolatruc. In the first 18 months after the formal telemarketing program was put into effect, more than 10,000 appointments had been set up for the BI Rolatruc sales force. The company recently had an up-to-date database of some 70,000 prospects and customers.[5]

You can see the power of using the phone for setting up your appointments. After you have done your initial cold calling by telephone, you are in a position to set up qualified appointments. You can set up the appointment for either an in-person visit or your next telephone call. Certain types of products are more easily sold when presented in person because you must demonstrate them. This approach is useful for selling office equipment, for example. Once a qualified prospect sees how the machine or the process works, closing the sale becomes easier.

The one-call/appointment technique can be broken down into three different subgroups, based on the place where the appointment will actually take place. These three variations are:

1. on the prospect's premises. This variation applies more to small office equipment and many business and personal services, such as insurance, home improvements, and the like.

2. on your home office premises. This variation applies more when you are selling the total facilities, such as the services

[5]Tony Light, "BI Rolatruc's In-House Telemarketing: The First 18 Months," *Industrial Marketing Digest* (UK) 13, no. 4 (Fourth quarter, 1988): 119–127.

of a printing house, video or audio production studio, hotel or meeting facility, and all types of manufacturing operations. As a rule, when the equipment is too large to transport to the client, the client needs to be transported to the showroom. This variation must be used when selling a service in which the facilities themselves are the product. Apartment complexes, health clubs, dance schools, and weight control programs are examples. Even real estate falls into this area because, if you think about it, you are setting up an appointment to show a home. In this circumstance, both customer and agent meet at a location other than that of the customer's home. When you require the customer to visit you for your appointment, it is a little more of a challenge than if you can go to the customer.

3. by phone only, with neither customer nor salesperson leaving their respective locations. This approach is much more difficult.

Since the phone-only approach usually requires many more contacts, both by phone and mail, it is more in line with some of the multiple-call approaches you will read about later in this book. An example of using the phone-only approach can be found at a successful video duplicating company with plants in a number of cities in the Midwest and its main office in the Detroit area. One of the company's more aggressive sales reps was given a territory where there was no plant. The other sales reps used a call/appointment approach to get the qualified prospect to the plant. Once on home turf, they could easily impress a client with their impressive facilities.

But what do you do when it is your job to get business from territories with no plant? It was certainly out of the question to fly most prospects in to see the facilities. So the sales rep improvised. He produced a videotape that simulated an in-person visit. Granted, the video could in no way make the same impact as seeing the equipment firsthand, but it did allow the rep to demonstrate his company's abilities in person on a video machine at the prospect's office.

The sales rep's videotape approach became so fine tuned that he was eventually able to send the tape on its own with some promotional material and use the phone to follow up. He was able to get orders from new clients without even having to visit the client in person! So, in a way, the one-call/appointment approach served as a beginning step to a more sophisticated approach later.

One salesperson we know in Chicago sells industrial packaging materials and machines. The major part of his selling effort is one of expanding orders from existing customers. His toughest part of the sale process is opening a new account, even if the initial order is very small. Once in the front door, however, he builds a good rapport and bends over backward to please his new customer. After he does get a first order, he handles the bulk of his selling effort for that client over the phone. He may have to visit that client no more than once a year. Even though he sees the client in person very seldom, he is in constant contact with his clients by telephone. There is no way he could have that much frequency of contact with all his clients if he relied primarily on in-person visits.

The one-call/appointment strategy is an approach that lends itself to selling former buyers or past clients. We saw a great example of this while conducting a program for the National Marine Manufacturers Association. We conducted a workshop for a group of their members' retail dealers at their annual trade show. While preparing for the program, we reviewed the research available and made an interesting discovery. The association's research projects showed that 8 percent of existing boat owners were in the market for a new boat.

We assumed that it was likely, therefore, that about 8 percent of each participant's customer list was also in the market for a new boat. Their number one concern was how to advertise to get in new customers, without spending a fortune. Ironically, one of their best sources of new business was already at their disposal. To get an idea of how this source would work for the group, we asked them to tell us how many customers they had. Most agreed on an average of 3,000. That being the case, they could assume that there were about 240 potential buyers in those 3,000 names. Their first task would be to use a tele-selling approach to contact those 3,000 people and invite them into the dealership to look at their new product lines. Not only should they be able to reach the 240 self-proclaimed potential buyers, but there likely would be a few more. After all, contacting the remaining 2,760 past customers who were not in the market could plant some seeds. After this section of the workshop, you could see the light bulbs going on over the retail dealers' heads. Following up with past customers just made good sense.

Two-Call-Close Strategy

The two-call-close strategy is required when your product or service requires a more involved selling process than a single phone call. It works very much like the one-call/appointment strategy, however. When you make the appointment after qualifying your lead, you are setting up a *telephone* appointment.

Closing over the phone appears to be more difficult than closing in person and in most cases it probably is. Yet, once you learn how to close on the phone, a whole new world opens up for you. Cold calling over the phone allows you to make four to five times as many cold calls in a given time. Now imagine the power of making sales presentations over the phone. Done properly, you get the same time-saving benefits.

The two-call close is most effective when you are selling a mid-range low-ticket product or service that your prospect is somewhat familiar with. By *mid-range* we mean items that usually cost between a few hundred or a few thousand dollars, depending on what it is and the marketing you are selling to. The dollar range suggested here is only a guideline. You may find that your product or service requires a two-call-close approach, yet it may sell for $20 or $20,000. Every circumstance is unique, so always take these suggestions as just that: suggestions. Feel free to modify, adapt, and improve where necessary to make these ideas work well for you.

The major difference between the two-call and one-call approaches is that the product or service sold with the two-call approach usually requires that the customer receive something in the mail as a follow-up before he or she is in a posture to buy. The one-call approach, on the other hand, is best used for a product or service that is low in price and easily understood.

Difficulty may arise when trying to figure out which of these two approaches to use. The most common setback is when unseasoned tele-sellers insist on using the two-call approach where the one-call approach would work. If they have not honed their tele-selling skills well enough, they may feel that sending out information helps them get more closes. For the really low-ticket items, however, the effect is just the opposite. So be careful. If you are seriously considering a two-call approach, make sure you should not be doing it all in just one phone call instead.

What *mid-range low ticket* usually means is that an *initial* purchase does not have to be very expensive. However, by opening up the account, you will have the opportunity for some very large sales over time. Such is the case with the video production house mentioned earlier. The first sale may be under $500—not a big commitment going in, at all. Yet, if the client likes the work and the service, there are opportunities for tens of thousands of dollars in sales on a regular basis.

Other examples of the initial, lower low-ticket and mid-range low-ticket sales areas may include printing; investments; insurance products; advertising; office supplies; automotive service; equipment upgrades, add-ons or peripherals; home or office maintenance and some improvements; and the like. In each of these categories, the buyer can "try" the new company with minimal risk. If for some reason he or she does not like the relationship, it can be broken very easily and a return can be made to the original suppliers. By the same token, this approach makes it much easier to give someone else a try. In these kinds of sales, the service and follow-up after the sale are just as important, if not more important, than getting the initial order.

So when using this approach, your first call qualifies the lead so you know that your prospect is in a position to buy what you have. Then you should follow up by sending some information about your product or service in the mail, along with some simple, fill-in-the-blank order forms and other background information. On your next call, you are ready to close the sale and take the order over the phone.

STREETSMART TELE-SELLING SECRET #2

In most selling situations, you can get a better return on your investment, in both money and time, if you use mail as follow-up *after* a tele-selling phone call, rather than as a softener *before* the phone call.

Another variation of the two-call approach is to develop a strategy of using a one-call-close system but adding a second call to those who have turned you down the first time. Similarly, you can use the second call as a follow-up to your first call and up-sell into something else. One recent test of this technique involved fund raising, and it produced some very interesting results. According to an article in *Fund Raising Management*, data from a telemarketing analysis were used to determine the effects of the program on donors who did not return their contributions in telephone-coded envelopes. The telemarketer made calls over a 60-day period to previous donors asking for an additional contribution. A follow-up letter was sent to those who made or had considered making a pledge. Three weeks later, a letter was sent: (1) to those who had pledged but made no donation, (2) to the "maybes", and (3) to the 8,177 actual donors. After six weeks, the entire file of 25,600 completed calls was matched against the file of donor activity. As a result of the telemarketing program, 80 percent of those who made pledges honored their commitment and 12 percent of those who said no sent a contribution. Furthermore, after a telephone call, 23 percent of those who had already contributed made an additional commitment. Perhaps the lesson to be learned here is that gold may be mined from "dead" leads, using a modified two-call-close strategy.[6]

Three-Call-Plus/Phone Close Strategy

The three-call-plus/phone-close technique is the one used most often by professional sales people who sell by telephone. This technique requires a little more patience because you must build the sale properly. But your close ratio over the phone can be much better.

The term *three-call-plus close* can be a little misleading, unless you place emphasis on the "plus" part of it. You likely will find that you have to make perhaps dozens and dozens of calls before you are in a position to close a sale. "Three-call" refers to the *minimum* number of calls you have to make before you are even in a position to close the sale.

The title of this technique is somewhat misleading, because the telephone is not the only marketing tool you are using to get the

[6]Bruce R. McBrearty, "What Is the Effect of a Phone Call on Your Contribution," *Fund Raising Management* 17, no. 3 (May 1986): 94–95.

sale. You will use mail follow-ups also. Here is how the three-call-plus close strategy works:

The first call is used to qualify your lead and set up an appointment for the second call. You also get the prospect's commitment to review your background information before the second call. You then send a mailer containing a general brochure about your business and perhaps a few other promotional pieces to help build your credibility. It is important, however, that this material contain very little nuts-and-bolts information. Instead, it should focus only on benefits and include no information on prices or technical specifications.

As opposed to advertising-first strategists, the three-call people never use their direct-mail advertising as a softener. Rather, they call first and mail second. The reasoning behind this is simple: When you do a mailing with the intention of following up with phone calls, you waste much effort and money. If, in fact, you do plan to follow up with phone calls, you will find that most people never recall getting your mail piece. As a result, the prospect expects you to send another. This time it goes Federal Express. Besides the increased expense, you are also wasting valuable time.

Furthermore, the mass mailer most likely has a very small readership. Let's say you mail 1,000 pieces. You will be lucky to get 50 people even to look at it. On the other hand, if you call first, you will have an opportunity to talk to most of those 1,000 leads and find the ones who qualify and who want to review your printed material.

The second phone call is used to probe deeper into the needs of your prospect. You ask questions and listen closely to the answers. You begin to better understand your prospect's specific needs and problems. At that point, you are ready to start to set up the close. The next mail piece goes out. This one is more detailed. It contains more reinforcement material, more information about the product or service. It also includes a fill-in-the-blank form or worksheet, price sheet, contracts, order forms, and everything you need to put in their hands to get the sale—but still no specific information. The blanks are where the prices go.

You then make your third phone call at the appointed time. Now you are in a position to get the sale. You have had two phone contacts with the prospect, plus two follow-up contacts by mail. By the third contact, you are no longer a stranger. You have built rapport and established credibility with your prospect. You can now try to close the sale. Of course, you may not close the sale on the third call. As a matter of fact, it may take you another dozen calls to close—that is the reason for the "plus" in this strategy's name. But at least you have all of the elements in place, so that once your prospect is ready, so are you.

We usually use the three-call-plus/phone-close approach when selling our consulting and speaking services. These programs can range anywhere from thousands of dollars to many tens of thousands of dollars, and they are all closed with a series of phone calls and follow-up mailings. This strategy can also be very effective when selling high-ticket products and services, such as insurance, investments, real estate, cars, office machines, and industrial supplies of all kinds.

We sometimes use a hybrid of the two-call and three-call programs for one of the products we offer: an audio and video training package that is relatively inexpensive when compared to our consulting services. This package allows us to get a small sale in two calls and also to set ourselves up for a bigger sale in later calls. We have found that a prospect may sound very serious about investing in our services. Yet, if they balk at an initial $300 package, they are probably not really interested in a consulting program that could easily run six figures. So in this way we use a small initial investment as a qualifying technique. You may not have a smaller-ticket item to sell up front, but if you do, consider using it as a good door opener to develop a bigger sales relationship.

Also keep in mind that you can mix and match any of the various approaches. They are not set in cement. One client of ours sells franchises by using a hybrid of the advertising-first and three-call-close approaches. Their main form of advertising is handled by a public relations firm in Chicago. The PR firm arranges interviews with the news media in each of the markets where the company wants to sell its franchises. The company thus gets many thousands of dollars' worth of free media exposure in local newspapers, radio, and television, plus an occasional hit on a national level.

Exposure in the *news* media carries greater impact than exposure in the advertising media. News exposure generates more credibility. The company mentioned above qualifies prospects from the news-generated call-ins, then begins its three-call-plus/close process. When you are talking to people about investing their life savings into a new business venture, you can expect a sale to make many phone calls. And although the commitment is made on the phone, the soon-to-be franchisees must still fly to the home office to close the deal.

Telephone calls are only half of an effective teleselling program. Just as important are the printed follow-ups you send after each of the phone calls. We will now explain what you should send in your mail follow-up that will help position your final phone call for a close.

In the two-call approach, you are encouraged to send a special "teaser" mailing. In this mail packet, you should have some of the following items:

- general company brochure
- personal fact sheet
- publicity reprints
- testimonial letter reprints
- customized cover letter

The teaser mailing packet is described in detail in Chapter 4.

General Company Brochure

Enclose a brochure that explains some of the technical specifications of your product or service. Most companies, vendors, and manufacturers provide professionally produced promotional pieces. But you do not want to stop there. The brochure you use should be customized for your client. Those beautiful, slick brochures do not always get read, so write notes to your client in the margins. Underline or highlight key points in the copy. Use small adhesive slips to make other notes. Take the gorgeous printed piece and make it ugly, noticeable, and personal.

Personal Fact Sheet

Provide your qualified prospect with some background about you as the sales representative. This can be a single sheet with a list of your accomplishments and perhaps a photo. You should list anything that gives you credibility and portrays you as a responsible, reliable person. You should come across as a person with whom they would like to develop a strong business relationship. Use a resume format if you like, but do not be too technical. Sell yourself as if you are applying for a job, because in a sense you are.

Testimonial Letters

Testimonial letters from clients are invaluable in establishing your reputation. Ideally, you want them addressed to you. (Later in this book you will learn how to go about getting these letters.) Even if these letters are addressed to the company, however, they can help you build your credibility. Highlight just a few of the key phrases in each letter, using a brightly colored highlighter.

Publicity Reprints

If you or your company has received some favorable publicity, include reprints of these articles in your "adver-teaser." Just as you did with your recommendation letters, highlight key phrases in the article. You will learn how to generate this publicity for yourself in a later chapter.

Customized Cover Letter

A customized letter to your prospect is important. This is most effective when done on a word processor, so that your prospect's name and company can be mentioned throughout the letter, even though the basic letter itself is boilerplate.

In all, your "adver-teaser" should consist of about four to eight pieces. Include no specific or detailed information about pricing. At this point your mail packet should be more fluff than stuff. You do not yet want to provide your prospect with enough information to make a decision.

More details about how to write the letters and construct the special mail packets are given in later chapters. For now, let's move on to the ultimate form of StreetSmart Tele-Selling: making and closing the sale completely on the phone. If you can do that, you can make any of the other approaches work, as well. Granted, this last approach takes a great deal of skill and effort. Yet, once you master it, you will have the ability to generate three to four times more total sales than you previously may have produced.

This ultimate approach is known as *three-call-plus selling*. When done properly, it can take your tele-selling all the way from prospecting, qualifying, and setting appointments to getting the order. The three-call-plus approach follows the same procedures as the approaches already mentioned, then continues where they leave off. During your third telephone call, you must probe for even more detailed information. Your goal is to uncover details of what it is going to take to win your client over. You must determine what you have to provide to give your customer exactly what he or she wants and needs.

This probing is particularly important when you have to work with many variables. An example is an advertising sales campaign, where the customer has many components to consider, such as:

- the size of the ad,
- the frequency or number of times it runs,
- when it appears,
- what section of the publication, and
- whether it runs in black and white, two colors, or full color.

In your third phone call, you should work with the fill-in-the-blank papers you sent in the second mail follow-up before the third phone call. You must also handle any final objections and close the sale. Then, while still on the phone, you should guide your prospect through the process of completing the fill-in-the-blank paperwork. Finally, you will direct the prospect to send the approved papers back to you (preferably with payment enclosed!). Even though this sales process is called the three-call-plus approach, it may require anywhere from 5 to 10 calls, perhaps even more, to finalize a sale.

Taking Care of Business

Consider the predicament of Jeffrey and his partner Ed: Just out of college, they started a small business selling "CARE" packages to the parents of college students. It is a competitive service that is offered by some student organizations on campus, as well. However, until Jeff and Ed jumped in, nobody had developed and promoted student "CARE" packages on a national level.

There are a couple of different ways to approach this type of business. The most obvious is to buy a direct-mail list of the parents of college freshmen. The other approach is to get the schools officially behind the program and help with the marketing. After all, they have mailing lists and do mailings to parents with some regularity.

Jeff and Ed tried to enlist the aid of the admissions department by offering a percentage of sales to the appropriate campus organization. Their first approach was to send out letters to deans. No response. They mailed again. No response again. It was time to get StreetSmart.

They got on the phone using the 20-second opener described on pages 47–50 in Chapter 3. They talked to the deans, qualified them, then sent background material about the program. Next they did a follow-up call to get the deans' reaction to the program. Some agreed on the second call, while others needed a little more thinking time. Apparently, one of the inherent dangers of working with college administrators is that they insist on thinking about things. As a follow-up to their phone calls, Jeff and Ed shipped each qualified dean a full-size sample of their "CARE" package!

In their first year, Jeff and Ed got more than 70 major colleges and universities to go on their program. In exchange for a small percentage of sales donated to student programs, they received a full endorsement from each school. In addition, many of the schools mailed announcements about the program to parents and included a letter from a dean. Some schools even included Jeff's and Ed's full-color brochure, showing all of the different "CARE" packages from which the parents could choose. The orders came in either by mail or on a toll-free number. With the phone-in orders, of course, Jeff and Ed had an opportunity to up-sell into additional packages for events later in the year (i.e., birthdays, mid-term examinations, etc.).

On both the mail-in orders and the call-in orders, Jeff and Ed had an opportunity to ask for referrals of other parents. For these new prospects, they had the option of mailing the brochure or calling them directly.

Their StreetSmart approach not only illustrates the power of using the phone to get the deans to participate, but, because of the direct personal contact, Jeff and Ed were able to get the schools to do the mailings and give an endorsement, as well. Try and do that with junk mail!

More Three-Call Variations

Once you put a three-call-plus close strategy to work, you may find that you need to modify it slightly as you gain experience. We found that many of our clients, once qualified on the first phone call, were far enough along in their decision-making process that they required our full information kit. Sending the adver-teaser first sometimes annoyed them. So, we started experimenting with sending out the more expensive information kit after the first phone call.

This process worked well, yet it did cause a few problems. One problem was that some of the qualified prospects did not recall getting the info kit when we asked about it during the second phone call. To help draw more attention to the info kit after the first phone call, we first sent out a notice to the client. It was printed on 8½-inch-by-5½-inch textured card stock, folded to look like an invitation. The envelope was hand addressed and was posted with a commemorative first class stamp. There was no return address. Because it did not look like a solicitation, its readership was very high.

When you opened the envelope, the cover of the "announcement" was a two-color cover with our logotype. The message on the inside was printed on the word processor and read:

> Dear (prospect's first name):
>
> In just a few days you will be receiving our "Streetfighter's" Information Kit which has been specifically assembled for you as you requested in our phone call. In it you will find some very interesting background information about our program which we customized to suit your needs.
>
> You will easily recognize it as it will arrive by UPS in a large, 9-x-12, black envelope. Our oversized mailing label features a bold-red "Streetfighter" logo in a black pennant. We look forward to getting your feedback on the information.
>
> Sincerely,

This announcement goes out via the postal service within 24 hours after the first phone call. The info kit is then shipped out two days later via UPS. Even though we are making fewer contacts before the prospect receives the info kit, the announcement is a low-cost and effective way to help create awareness and anticipation of the more expensive info kit. A similar effect could be accomplished by sending out a good-quality post card, instead of an announcement in an envelope.

The other problem we noticed when using the three-call-plus close strategy was that we often had difficulty getting in touch with the client on the second phone call. This seemed odd to us since they readily took our first phone call. Apparently, once they received the info kit, they knew they had initiated a buying sequence. Since they probably felt that some kind of decision was inevitable, they started to feel uncomfortable when the second call arrived.

We stayed with it, making four or more phone calls until finally they would get on the line and talk to us. Usually there was some resistance, but in some of the conversations, we were able to move the prospects along, while others were disqualified. Either outcome was acceptable because we had movement.

To make the second contact easier, we sent out another notice. This notice was sent only after we had called at least six times over a two-week period with no response. As before, the notice looked like an invitation so that it had a greater chance of being opened and read. There was no return address; it was hand written; and, again, we used a first-class, commemorative stamp. The notice read:

Dear (prospect's first name):

This is a bribe! I want to give you a copy of Jeff Slutsky's book *Streetfighting*, free. Here is the catch: I have tried at least a half-dozen times to talk to you and get your honest feedback on the information you received about our program.

I'm sure your busy schedule makes it difficult for you to answer everybody's calls. However, if you will personally give me a call right now and give me your feedback on the material, I will send you an autographed copy of Jeff's book, free. I want your feedback regardless of what it is. But you and I need to have one brief conversation, and I will send the book off to you right away.

Call me right now at 614/443-5555. If I'm not available, I will return the call, and the deal still stands. Call me.

Sincerely,

(sales rep's name)

Experiment with variations of these ideas and discover for yourself what works best for you.

A three-call-plus strategy takes more effort than other approaches. But initially you can work it in combination with some of the other strategies with which you feel more comfortable. By using this approach, you can develop important telephone skills that help you improve your sales.

2

Getting Past
the Gatekeeper

All the sales techniques are worthless unless you get to communicate with the decision maker. Unfortunately, there is usually a buffer or filter between you and the person who makes the buying decisions. That buffer may be a secretary, an assistant, or some other "gatekeeper" who has the ability to keep you from talking to the right person.

The Five Variables

There are many ways of dealing with the gatekeeper. The approach you use, and how successful you are, often depends on a number of influences. These variables may include:

1. your own personal selling style,
2. the personality of the gatekeeper,
3. the specific product or service you sell,
4. the organization or prospect type you sell to, and
5. the relationship between the gatekeeper and decision maker.

Though the gatekeeper may be tough to get past, this difficulty can be made to work to your advantage. It has often been suggested that the tougher the gatekeeper, the easier the decision maker. Once past a tough gatekeeper, you may discover you have an easier task getting the sale. Thus, the key is knowing how to get past the gatekeeper.

The gatekeeper is potentially dangerous to your sales success, because he or she cannot say yes but can say no. It is the gatekeeper's job to screen calls. If this person allowed every salesperson who called to talk to the decision maker, very little work would be accomplished. So the gatekeeper tries to make sure that the few calls that do get through are important. Your objective is to impress the gatekeeper with the importance of your call; however, make sure that you give the absolute minimum amount of information required to talk to the decision maker.

It is often difficult to describe the relationship between the decision maker, the gatekeeper, and the salesperson. But, while watching a Monday night football game recently, a suitable comparison finally hit us. The color commentator was drawing plays on the TV screen, and many of those plays seemed to parallel the different strategies that can be used to reach the decision maker through a gatekeeper.

Here is how the football analogy works: You are the quarterback, and it is your job to get the ball to the end zone and score a touchdown. You have many different strategies to help you do it, but the biggest obstacle between you and the end zone is a tough defensive line, represented by the gatekeeper. The gatekeeper's job is to keep you from reaching the end zone, and he or she will do anything possible to protect the goal line.

In your mental huddle, you must decide which play to use to get the ball past the defensive line. Your options are:

1. a run up the middle,
2. an end run,
3. a reverse,
4. a quarterback sneak,
5. a bomb,
6. a fake punt,
7. a real punt, and
8. a screen pass.

The Run Up the Middle

The run up the middle is the most direct approach and, when done properly, it can be your most effective approach. The reason for its higher rate of success is that you can have one or more verbal "blockers" helping you. This "offensive line" will help you bob and weave your way to the goal.

STREETSMART TELE-SELLING SECRET #3

Never try to sell your product or service to buffers or filters. Only sell them on putting you through to the decision maker.

The key point in the run-up-the-middle strategy is that you must not put yourself in the vulnerable position of selling your product or service to a secretary. Because the secretary is not the decision maker, you will waste your time and put yourself in the position of never being able to get through. On the other hand, if you can turn the secretary into a blocker for your side, she or he will actually run interference for you and help you get through.

Figure 2-1   "Run up the middle" is the most direct approach.

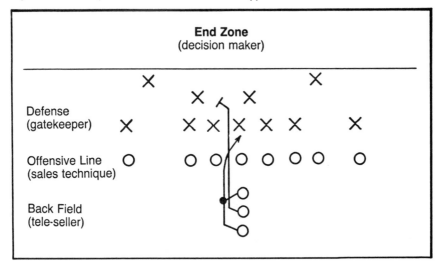

A good screener will ask you many questions to get as much information as possible before allowing you to talk to the boss. To shift sports briefly, it is like an oral game of tennis, with you serving and the secretary returning the volley with a question.

The person who asks the questions controls the conversation. (Later in this book you will learn in greater detail how to use this principle in talking with prospects.) There are several reasons for this. First, by asking a question, you force the other person to pay attention to you. If you merely talk, the listener's mind can wander and think about other things. But the minute you say, "Let me ask you this . . . ," the listener must pay attention, because a response will be required. This reflex is automatic.

Second, a person can speak at a rate of about 250 words a minute, while a person who is listening can think at about 2,000 words a minute. Of course, these averages are rough: If you are from New York, you might talk at 350 words a minute with gusts up to 400; if you are from the South, you might be slower. Yet, you can think about seven to eight times as fast as you can talk. So, whenever you are talking to a prospect, keep in mind that he or she has a great deal more time to think of reasons *not* to buy from you. By asking questions and letting the prospect do the talking, you have the advantage of thinking many times faster than the prospect can.

Third, when you ask a question, you show empathy and concern for the need of the prospect. Perhaps the most important aspect of asking questions is that it allows you to get valuable information from the prospect. You can discover what your prospect's needs really are. People love to talk about themselves, so let them, and, in the process, gather all the other information you can.

When you ask a question, you have to remember that people respond with an appropriate response. This means that if someone asked you "How much is this?" which is an information question, you would not respond with yes. That response would be inappropriate to an information-seeking or open-ended question.

These same principles apply when you are talking to the gatekeeper. You want to remain in control, and it helps for you to ask the questions. You want very little information from the gatekeeper, but you do want him or her to take a specific action. And that action is to put you through to the decision maker.

By using questions, *you* control your conversation with the gatekeeper. At the same time, you must use questions differently from the way you would with your prospect. When talking with the gatekeeper, you respond *to a question,* but you follow up *with a command.* Then *you* use the question to confirm that they understand your command.

STREETSMART TELE-SELLING SECRET #4

When you are being screened by a gatekeeper, follow up every question that you answer with a command statement to put you in touch with the prospect.

For example, when you ask, "Is Mr. Herman in, please?" that is a question that requires a yes or no response. Likewise, when you follow it up with, "May I speak to him?" you are in effect asking the secretary's permission to speak to the boss. That question also gives the secretary the opportunity to say no. Those types of questions put your gatekeeper in control over you.

You can turn that control around by giving an order, thus avoiding being in a position of asking for permission. When you combine the order with a firm but pleasant pitch in your voice, you come across in a more authoritative manner and increase your chances of getting through.

Secretaries know that part of their job is to screen calls. Often, they do not feel they have done their job suitably unless they ask some questions. The degree to which screeners feel you must be screened often depends on the wishes of their decision makers as well.

The screeners feel that the more questions you are asked, the better they are doing their job. Therefore, secretaries will often ask you many questions, regardless of how trivial some of those questions may be. Only after these secretaries feel that they have done their jobs properly—provided you have not given them any information that allows them to decide not to let you speak to the decision maker—do you stand a chance of getting through. So you must always remember *not* to volunteer any more information than the absolute minimum needed to satisfy the filter's questions.

STREETSMART TELE-SELLING SECRET #5

> Give the gatekeeper only the absolute minimum amount of information needed to answer his or her questions.

Finally, never lie. If you lie to a secretary, you lose all your credibility. I know that some salespeople have used some fairly tall tales to get through to a prospect, and I am going to share some of the more, shall we say, creative ones later in this chapter just for your amusement. You are much better off when you are not lying. Just provide the bare minimum amount of information. The less information the gatekeeper has, the better your chances of getting through to the prospect.

Keeping all of this in mind, here is an example of a conversation between Marc Slutsky, a seasoned StreetSmart Tele-Seller, and a seasoned gatekeeper:

"Mr. Herman's office."
"Did you say that this is Mr. Herman's office?"
"Yes, I did."
"Great. Who am I speaking to?"
"This is Stacy."
"Oh, Stacy. Please put me through to Mr. Herman."
"Who's calling?"
"Marc Slutsky. Please let Mr. Herman know I've called."
"And who are you with?"
"RMI. Please tell Mr. Herman I'm holding long distance for him."

At this point, the questions start getting a little more difficult to answer. You may not feel totally comfortable with some of these responses, but they have been effective in getting to talk to a decision maker.

"Is he expecting your call?"
"I don't believe we have set up a specific time, but please let him know I am on the line."
"And what is it regarding?"

"Let Mr. Herman know that I have the answers to the marketing questions. He is supposed to be in, isn't he?"

"Does he know you?"

"You know, I don't think we have met personally, Stacy, but I do have that information for him, so please let him know I've called. Okay?"

This is an extreme case, but let's examine why Marc used the particular answers to the questions this secretary gave him.

First, when Marc called, he tried to get the name of the gate-keeper, and you will notice that he used it a few times throughout the conversation. People love to hear that their own names. It helps break down some of their resistance as well.

Also notice that Marc gave minimal information in answering each of her questions. He did not even offer his name until she specifically asked for it. By allowing her to ask a lot of questions, she feels she did her job of screening him properly. At the same time, Marc did not put the conversation in jeopardy by giving her enough information to make a decision not to let him through.

After the first few exchanges, he always followed up with a question to regain control and to get affirmation that she understood his request to put him through. Her later questions were more difficult to answer. She was really trying to dig in and find out the purpose of his call. If Marc responded with something like "it's about advertising," "insurance," or "investments," she could easily have said that her boss was not interested. To avoid that, Marc played a little word game. He told her that he had the answer to the marketing questions. That is true. No matter what question the prospect might have had about marketing, Marc had the answer to it. She may have interpreted that statement as meaning that they had been working together before or that this call was in response to some previous meeting, but he did not lie.

Marc used the same approach when she asked him if her boss knew him. If he had responded with "No, but I would like to talk to him about some stocks," there would have been no way to get through. On the other hand, Marc responded with, "Well, I don't believe we have met personally, but I do have that information for him." You can see what kind of impression that makes. Did Marc say he knew him? No, he answered the question without telling a lie.

As you can see, it is not so much what you say, but rather what you do not say. I like to refer to this communication technique as "creative avoidance."

Warning: some salespeople are disturbed or even offended by this approach. You should use it only if you feel comfortable with it. If it makes you feel that you are trying to deceive the gatekeepers, do not use it. On the other hand, if you find that you are not getting through enough of the time, you might give it a try to see how it works for you. After giving it a good shot for a couple of days, you can always try another approach or go back to what you were doing before.

The End Run

Sometimes you just cannot get past the gatekeeper, so it becomes necessary to try the end run to get around the defensive line. Here are a couple of ways to get around the gatekeeper when it is reasonably certain you will not be able to work your way through.

Some business people have direct lines. Try calling the receptionist first and asking for your prospect's extension number, and you might be able to bypass the gatekeeper altogether.

Figure 2-2   The "end run" allows you to go around the gatekeeper.

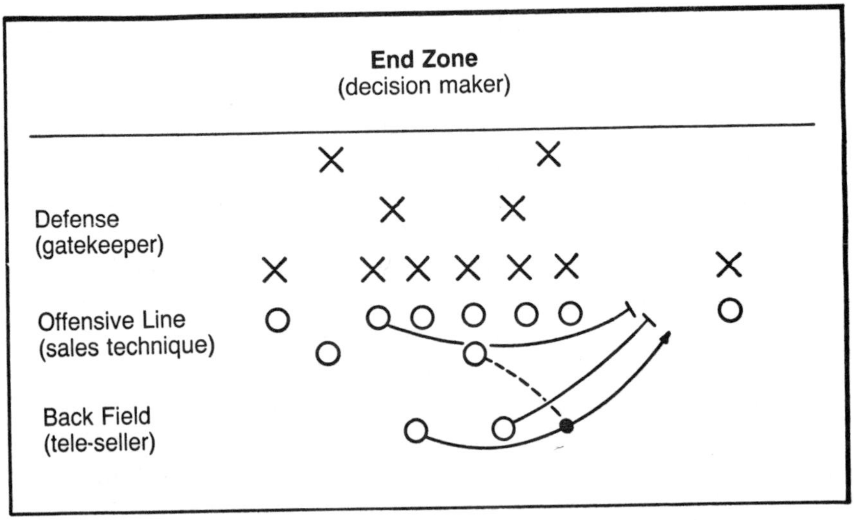

Another end-run approach is to call an entirely different department than the one you want. Say, for example, you want to call Mr. Oppenheimer in Accounts Payable and cannot seem to get past the gatekeeper. Try calling someone in shipping and ask for Mr. Oppenheimer. They will tell you that you have reached the wrong department. Ask them to transfer you directly to Mr. Oppenheimer's office. They sometimes have a corporate directory with all of the extension numbers and can put you right through.

The Reverse

In football, the reverse often works because the ball carrier comes at the defense from an unexpected direction. The reverse also works in tele-selling. With this technique, you call the office of someone higher up in the organization. If you are trying to reach the executive vice president, for example, then you call the chief executive officer's office. The CEO's secretary will inform you that you have reached the wrong office and will usually offer to transfer you to the right party. A call transferred from the boss's office stands a little better chance of getting through.

Figure 2-3   The "reverse" allows you to get transferred by your prospect's boss!

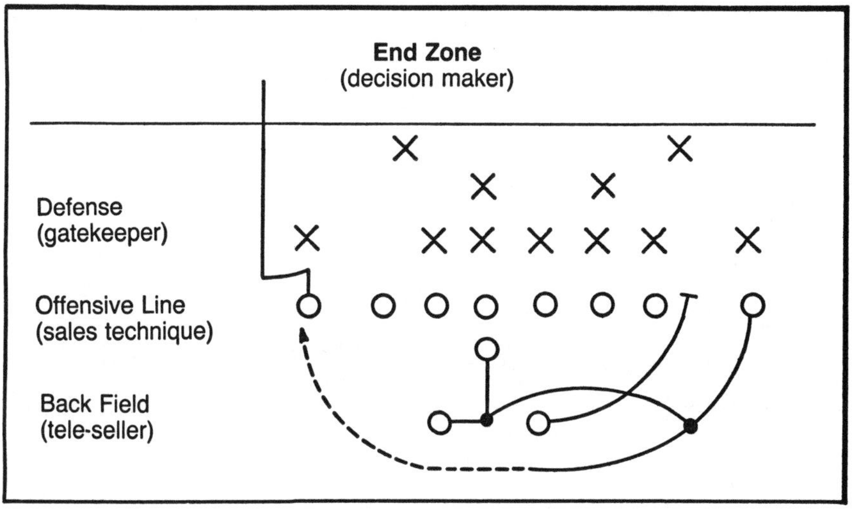

Calling people higher up also works nicely when you are not quite sure who is the best person to talk to about your product or service. Call the president and briefly explain to him or her the purpose of your phone call. Then ask for a recommendation of who is the best person for you to talk to about this particular area. Not only will you often get to the right person more easily, you will also make a very powerful impression by mentioning that, "Mr. Powers, the president, recommended that I call you directly." Of course, if the president personally transfers the call for you, your chances of getting through are even better.

The Quarterback Sneak

To run the quarterback sneak, try calling very early in the morning. Often, busy executives get to the office by six or seven in the morning, long before their secretaries show up. And, when their phones ring, there is a very good chance they will answer it themselves. The quarterback sneak can also work at lunchtime, after work, and on weekends. At lunchtime, you may be fortunate to have a substitute secretary filling in for the regular one while he or she gets something to eat. The fill-in filter is usually much easier to get past.

Figure 2-4   The "quarterback sneak" is when you call your prospect when the gatekeeper isn't there.

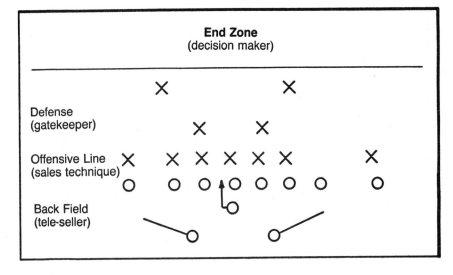

The Bomb

In football, this a usually a desperation move. The quarterback heaves the ball down the field as far as he can throw it and hopes it gets caught. Every once in a while, you will have no alternative. Time is running out on the clock. You are down by a couple of sales and for some reason every offensive move you've made has just not done the job. Now you throw the bomb—sometimes called the Hail Mary.

One tele-selling version of the bomb requires you to break StreetSmart Tele-Selling Secret #3. You have tried everything and the only way you are even going to get a shot at the decision makers is to sell the gatekeeper on the product or service. Chances for success are minimal, but if this is the only move you have left, you have to give it your best shot.

For some types of products and services, using the bomb is not quite as risky. We have noticed in our own office that one of our salespeople consistently works the bomb and does it very success-fully. Perhaps the reason for his success is due in part to his own personality. He has a great phone voice—very deep and authorita-tive, yet nonthreatening. He is also a charmer and very persistent, though not to the point of annoying a prospect or client.

Figure 2-5 The "bomb" is a desperation move.

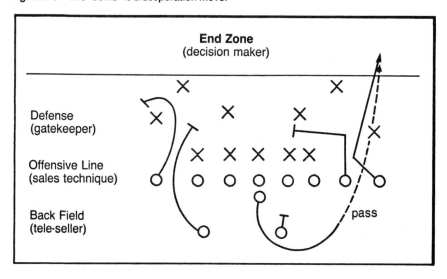

Be cautious using the bomb. It is often a disaster when the prospect perceives your offering as nonessential. The same caveat applies to oversaturated industries with a surplus of sales reps: Insurance or investments are two areas that come to mind. Yet, if all else fails, you might as well throw the bomb!

When You Bomb, Throw the Bomb

Another version of the bomb is to use direct mail or other standard approaches to sales after you have tried your best tele-selling approaches for getting past the gatekeeper. Eileen sells original art at an exclusive Midwest art gallery. One of her clients, an attorney, had recently purchased a Stobart print and suggested that she contact his partner. He had noticed another Stobart print—of Georgetown. Because he knew that his partner had gone to school there, he informed Eileen that if she merely made his partner aware of this print, he would buy it.

She tried many times to talk to the partner, but to no avail. She wanted to set up an appointment and bring the print in for him to see. No dice. After exhausting her tele-selling repertoire, she decided to break the teleselling rules and throw the bomb. Her bomb was to send the partner a letter and color catalogue with a picture of the Georgetown print. The next day, Eileen had a note on her desk informing her that an attorney had called and asked to have the print delivered.

In this unique situation, the product and the customer were so perfect for each other that simple awareness was all that was needed to get the sale. In this case, it was a mailer that helped her get past the gatekeeper.

Eyeball to Eyeball

A very creative way of getting past the gatekeeper was presented in an issue of *Sound Selling*.[1] One segment featured a salesperson of the month—in this particular issue, a very clever sales rep who sold products to eye doctors. There was one doctor whom the sales rep particularly wanted as a customer because the doctor

---

[1]*Sound Selling* is a monthly, audio-cassette, sales-oriented magazine published by Nightingale-Conant Corp., 7300 N. Lehigh Ave., Chicago, IL 60648. It consists of two cassette tapes and features a variety of authors, speakers, and sales trainers sharing their ideas on selling and related topics.

did a high volume and was respected by all the other ophthalmologists in the area.

He tried repeatedly to get in to see the doctor, but gatekeepers just would not let him have a shot. Neither efforts by phone nor in person worked. Finally, out of desperation, he set up an eye appointment. At his appointment, when he was face to face with the doctor, he told him that he really did not need an eye exam. He went on to say that since he was paying for the exam anyway, he would like to take an equivalent amount of time to explain his product. Taken aback by this unique approach, the doctor agreed. Once the doctor saw that the product was truly a superior one, the sale was made. He not only became a tremendous customer but has referred much business to the salesperson as a result of this effort. Had the sales representative not had the tenacity and chutzpah to try this approach, there never would have been an opportunity for a sale.

The Fake Punt

The fake punt's relationship to getting past the gatekeeper is not dissimilar to the relationship between closing techniques and specific closes like the "Colombo close" or the "doorknob close."

Figure 2-6   The "fake punt" is when you appear to give up and then you ask just one more question . . .

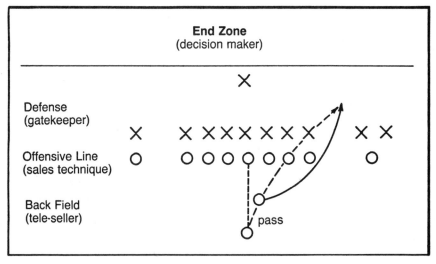

Simply, after you have failed in every attempt at reaching the decision maker, you concede to the gatekeeper that you give up. You have tried on numerous occasions to talk briefly with the decision maker, and it just seems that it is going to be impossible. Then you pause or perhaps sigh. At this point, the gatekeeper realizes that you give up. As a result, he or she is less guarded or defensive. The mental barriers weaken. Then, as an afterthought, you inquisitively query the gatekeeper: "Let me ask you something, just out of curiosity. What did I do wrong?" Your tone should be one of some sadness with a slight hint of confusion.

Sometimes the gatekeeper will begin to feel sorry for you and a little empathetic. He or she might respond with a little advice to try to cheer you up a little. The response may be, "What do you mean, what did you do wrong?" This gives you an opportunity to secure some sympathy.

"Well, I do not know really . . . except that I have this service that I believe strongly about. It is very good, and those who have told us they use it say they get excellent results. Now, I do not know for sure if it's appropriate for Mr. Smith or not. But, just suppose, on the off chance, that this does bring him the kind of success that it's done for so many others. It just seems a shame that he didn't at least have the opportunity to consider it. You know?"

You might just get the gatekeeper to let you talk to the boss.

The Real Punt

There is a time to be persistent, and then there is a time to say forget it and go on to the next prospect. When to punt is certainly a tough call to make, but generally you will find that you can punt a little more quickly in telephone sales than in field sales. There are many more prospects out there, and if you cannot get through to this one after you have given it the good old college try, it is time to punt and move on.

Even after you punt, you might want to throw the lead into your tickler file and call back in five or six months. Circumstances have a way of changing. People retire, move, get transferred, or quit. The next time you call, you may find a different game entirely.

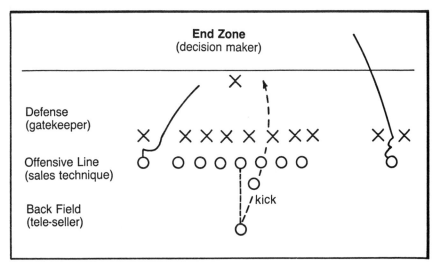

Figure 2-7   The "punt" is when you know it's time to give up and move on to more fertile pastures.

In contrast to a real game of football, where you score points when you reach the goal line, you do not always score in tele-selling when you get past the gatekeeper. Your tele-selling touchdown only gains you the opportunity to present your story to the prospect. That is when the real tele-selling begins.

The Screen Pass

The screen-pass technique is presented last because it deals with an entirely different type of gatekeeper: the decision influencer. The decision influencer, like the standard gatekeeper, also keeps you from talking directly to the decision maker. The difference with the influencer is that in most cases the decision maker delegates the responsibility for gathering information about the potential purchase to an assistant, who then becomes the decision influencer. The assistant compiles the information, forms an opinion, and presents it to the decision maker.

When dealing with an influencer, as opposed to an actual decision maker, you must accede to a weaker position for getting the sale and realize that getting the sale will be more difficult. Not

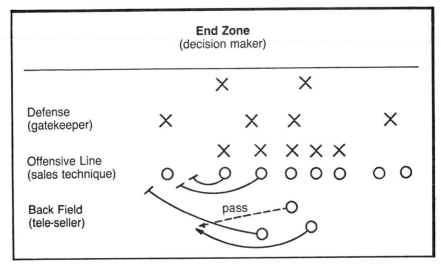

Figure 2-8   The "screen pass" is when an "influencer" carries the ball for you to get to the decision maker.

only will you have to sell your product or service to the influencer, but once the influencer "buys," you will also have to teach the influencer how to sell it, on your behalf, to the decision maker.

In many cases, the influencer serves as a go-between. At any rate, when you are in this kind of selling position, the gatekeeper is your ally. Keep in mind, however, that just because the influencer wants what you are selling does not mean you are going to get the sale. You have to provide your influencer with all the ammunition that he or she needs to convince the final decision maker that this is the right move. You, in effect, dump the ball off to this person, just as a quarterback looks long, finds every target covered, and lobs a short screen pass to one of his running backs.

Once you have sold the influencer on your product or service, it is very important that you find out how the final decision will take place. You need to know how the decision-making process works. For example, we might work with a national trade association that is considering our program for their annual convention. The association's programming committee has to approve or vote on whom they want. Committees are tough, because it is very difficult to control the sale. The buying decision is made by a group instead of an individual. The difficulty compounds itself when you do not have direct access to the committee. Instead, you have to work through an influencer who presents your case, on your behalf, to the group.

In this predicament, you may find it useful to learn some things about the committee, including its size, and when the members will meet to decide on your product or service. To help your influencer, provide him or her with enough sets of your promotional materials for each member of the committee. And you will make a much greater impression on committee members if you provide color brochures and quality reprints of testimonial letters displayed in a professional-looking folder. A committee reviewing a dozen poor-quality photocopies of material stapled together is less likely to be swayed in your favor.

You should also find out from your influencer, if possible, what some of the committee members' main objections are. They may have or take the time to review your material before the meeting, so consider contacting a few of the members for their feedback and possible objections. Then work with your influencer on how to handle those particular objections. This is important, because often the influencer is not a proficient salesperson and does not have the product knowledge that you do. So help prepare that influencer as strongly as you can.

This same approach works when the influencer is presenting to a single decision maker. Again, you must help your influencer present the information so that you are more likely to get a favorable response.

You may also find yourself dealing with an influencer when you have already talked to the decision maker. Your call allowed you to present to the boss, but then he or she referred you to the assistant who will handle the details. If your discussion with the boss went well, especially if it went well enough to get referred, then you are on strong ground. Seize the opportunity with the decision maker to find out what possible roadblocks might appear. Then, when you are working with the influencer, you can help him or her best prepare for the sale, provided you have sold the influencer on your product or service.

When selling items for the home, you often find that decisions are made jointly between husbands and wives. Though on the surface the decision appears to be made jointly, in actuality the balance of decision-making power is not equal. One of the two serves as the influencer while the other is either the final decision maker or the "vetoer." Whenever possible, try to get both on the line at the same time during your follow-up calls so that no matter which one is which, you have the ability to get a decision. You can really put a sale at jeopardy if you do not involve both the husband and wife. This is because the missing partner has the ability to take pot shots at your product or service.

3

Making Your Initial Contact with Your Prospect

STREETSMART TELE-SELLING SECRET #6

> Your initial telephone presentation opener, the first four sentences you speak, determines whether your prospect wants to listen to your presentation.

Once you are finally in a position to present directly to the decision maker, you have an entirely new challenge awaiting you. You now face the most critical part of selling over the phone—your opener. The opener is what happens in the first 10 to 20 seconds of talking directly with your prospect. In this chapter, you will discover some successful techniques for opening conversations with prospects.

STREETSMART TELE-SELLING SECRET #7

> Your first four sentences should consist of the following:
>
> 1. your introduction;
> 2. the benefits, solutions, or end results of using your products or services;

3. your new news; and

4. a negative question asking permission to make your presentation.

Your Introduction

Step one of your opener is to introduce yourself and the company you represent. One technique suggested for a more effective opener is repeating the prospect's name to make sure you do, in fact, have the right person on the line. Here is an example of the first line of the opener, using this approach.

"Mr. Herman (wait for a response such as 'Yes' or 'You got him.'), This is Jeff Slutsky with the Retail Marketing Institute in Columbus, Ohio."

In that first sentence, Mr. Herman has heard his name. He has also responded to the caller, which immediately involves him in the conversation. And, he knows who the caller is, what company or organization the caller represents, and from where the call is coming. The reason you mention the city is that long distance seems to add a sense of urgency and importance to the call. However, if you are making a local call, change the first sentence to something like this: "This is Jeff Slutsky from the Retail Marketing Institute here in Columbus." This approach works best when close proximity is an important feature to your prospect.

STREETSMART TELE-SELLING SECRET #8

If the name of your company telegraphs to your prospect your type of business, and if doing so might cause the wrong conclusion to be drawn about what benefits you really have to offer, use your company's initials in your opener.

Your Benefit Statement

Because Jeff's name or the company's name probably do not mean much to Mr. Herman, the second sentence explains in a very precise way the benefits of what we offer. We want to stress how we are unique. A good benefit statement, incidentally, is even more important if your company name is well known. This is because your prospect may think he or she already knows the purpose of your call and might try to cut you off before you get an opportunity to present your benefits.

You should immediately launch into the next sentence that explains what you do and why you are unique. In this sentence, you must provide the user benefits of what you do. In our case, we would *not* say "We conduct seminars, workshops, and consulting projects in local store marketing." That tells Mr. Herman just enough information so he can tell us he has no interest.

Instead, we stress the unique benefits of our products and services to the prospect. For example, we might say "We're specialists in the area of helping businesses learn how to advertise, promote, and generally increase sales without spending money."

Now that is a benefit. Notice that we did not mention anything about seminars or consulting. Those are details. How we do it is of little consequence. The fact that we offer these benefits or results is the key.

Your New News

In the third sentence you should present the "new news." We have to have a special reason for the phone call, one that creates a sense of urgency. It could be a new product or service you are introducing or a special introductory offer. You want to offer one more piece of news that sweetens the benefit to the prospect a little more. For example, we sometimes use something like this: "The reason I'm calling you is because we have recently developed some new techniques that many of our clients tell us are getting them tremendous response."

The Negative Question

Now, you are ready for the fourth and final sentence of your opener. In this sentence, you should ask the prospect's permission to continue the discussion. Therefore, the last sentence must be a question. And, because you are asking a question to get permission to do something, it must be a question that requires a yes or no response.

The problem is that almost everyone's natural reaction to a telephone solicitation is to say no. They want to say no. They are conditioned to say no. They are used to ill-trained script readers calling them up and boring them to death with a pitch like, "Hi. My name is Jeff. How are you doing today? We would like you to buy tickets to the circus . . ."

As soon as you start, their natural reaction is to say that they have no interest. "No, thanks anyway, but no." Because most of the people you are going to talk to on the phone are already preconditioned to say no in some fashion, you have to design the closing of your opener in a way that will get them to respond with a no. At the same time, by responding with a no, they will actually give an affirmative answer to your question and, therefore, give their permission to continue with the presentation.

Your ending question might be something like this: "Is there any reason why you wouldn't want to learn a little bit more about it?"

Notice that, when they respond with a no, they are giving you an affirmative answer to the question, and you can continue right on with the presentation. So, when you put it all together, it sounds like this:

"Mr. Herman (wait for him to respond), this is Jeff Slutsky of the Retail Marketing Institute in Columbus, Ohio. We're specialists in the area of helping businesses learn how to advertise, promote, and generally increase sales without spending a lot of money. The reason I'm calling you is that we have just developed some new techniques that our clients tell us are getting them some tremendous response. Is there any reason why you wouldn't want to learn a little more about it?"

"No."

"Great, let me ask you this . . ."

And you are right in the front door. It is that simple. You can change the wording to make the opener more comfortable for you, and of course you need to find just the right description of who you are and the new news you wish to present to your prospect.

Another approach you might try, depending on the type of product or service you sell, is to add another question in the middle of the opener. This works only if giving the name of your company will not deter your prospect from taking your phone call and if your company name is not too widely known. It goes like this:

"This is Jeff Slutsky of the Retail Marketing Institute. We specialize in teaching businesses how to advertise, market, and generally increase sales without spending a lot of money. We call our unique program Streetfighting. Have you heard of us? Well, like I said, we specialize in teaching low-cost promotional programs on the local level, and we have just developed some new techniques that many of our clients tell us are getting them some great results. Is there any reason why you wouldn't want to learn a little bit more about it?"

In this example, we sneak that extra question in: "Have you heard of us?" This brings the listener into the conversation sooner. It also is a nice piece of information to know, because every once in a while we get a yes. In that case, we follow up with, "No kidding. How do you know us?" We want to find out what they know, as well as how favorable the impression is, so we can proceed from there.

Usually, however, the answer is no. This answer gives us an opportunity to repeat and perhaps even refine or expand the benefit statement and then go on as we normally do. In the foregoing example, we stated that our program is done on a "local level." We also used both the company name and the product name. We find that more people know us or remember us as Streetfighters than as Retail Marketing Institute. As a result, we incorporated "Streetfighters" into the name, so that it is now "Streetfighter's Retail Marketing Institute." The point here is that you should make it easy for your prospects and customers to work with you. Give them what they want.

This approach might not be as effective, of course, if you are from American Express or AT&T, for example. Try calling up a prospect and telling them you are with American Express, then ask: "Have you heard of us?" You do *not* want to insult a prospect's intelligence and get off to a bad start.

Something you may want to try is to use the prospect's name two or three times in the opener. This is a technique suggested by our colleague and telemarketing expert, Stan Billue, author of *Double Your Income Selling on the Phone.* He feels that people just love to hear their own name and that by mentioning it three times in the first sentence, you will have a better response. It works this way:

"Mr. Herman, please."

"This is he."

"Mr. Jeff Herman?"

"Yes."

"Mr. Herman, my name is Jeff Slutsky with the Retail Marketing Institute and . . ."

Some tele-sellers find it a little difficult to repeat the prospect's name three times. Repeating the name just two times, however, seems to work fine, too. For example:

"Mr. Herman?"

"Yes."

"Mr. Herman, my name is Jeff Slutsky . . ."

Here are some other examples of effective openers. The first we developed for Central Greyhound Corporation.

"Mr. Brown? This is Bill Smith with the Doberman Package Express Service. We specialize in shipping time-sensitive packages the same day or the next day by 8:30 A.M. We have just initiated a new introductory program that allows you to save 60 percent for the next three months. Is there any reason why you wouldn't want to learn more about it?"

Notice that all four parts of the opener are there: introduction, description of the benefit, new news, and permission to continue.

Of course, you can change the elements in the opener at any time as new developments come up, but be careful not to pigeon-hole yourself. For example, assume that you just opened a new market. That is new news. The prospect you call may have no need for this new market, but could benefit from your service in other ways. By offering some new news that is too specific, he or she could turn you off. So, in the Greyhound example, it might be dangerous to use a new news sentence such as: "We've just started shipping directly to Obetz and Lima, Ohio." Such a statement gives your prospect the opportunity to respond with, "We never ship to those cities. Thanks anyway."

Make sure that your new news is something that cannot get you turned down. A special price reduction can be new news, provided you do not mention that it is on just a few items. New news could be any development or enhancement in service.

Another client in the discount motel business uses an appropriate opener geared for that particular market. When selling by phone to get corporate accounts, it sounds something like this:

"This is Bob Roberts with Marvelous Motor Inns here in Columbus. We specialize in providing high-quality, comfortable motel rooms at very competitive prices. Recently, we've introduced a special corporate discount program that saves you even more money. Is there any reason why you wouldn't want to learn more about it?"

By now you have the idea. You should create your own opener using the four steps just described.

As a professional salesperson selling quality products and services, you should be well-rehearsed and not need a script. But your opener *should* be scripted. And you should practice to the point that it does not sound as if you are reading it. It should sound unrehearsed and spontaneous.

The Five Tests for Qualifying Your Prospect

STREETSMART TELE-SELLING SECRET #9

When making your first telephone presentation to your prospect, your first objective is to qualify that prospect to see if it is worth your while to pursue doing business with this person.

Once you are in the front door, the most difficult part of your telephone selling effort has just begun. You now have permission to continue with the presentation, and your objective should be to determine whether you want to do business with this person. In other words, you need to qualify your prospect to see if there is potential for a sale.

STREETSMART TELE-SELLING SECRET #10

To qualify your prospects properly, you must find out if they pass certain qualifying tests. Each of these tests depends on your business and the type of product or service you sell. Most, however, include some variation of the following:

1. want,
2. need,
3. decision maker,
4. decision mode, and
5. budget or credit.

To qualify your prospect, you must ask a lot of questions to find out some important information. But what information do you need to know to qualify this prospect? In any business, there are many qualifiers that determine if you have the potential for getting a sale. However, you will often find that your prospect needs to pass five qualifiers or tests before you can make a commitment to pursue the sale. Of course, every type of business is different, and you may want to modify the list to best suit your particular needs. Use the five qualifiers given in the foregoing list as your starting point.

Want

The prospects have to want the benefit of what your product or service has to offer. If they do not want it, it is very hard to get a sale. Do not waste your time unless they want it.

Also, if you disqualify them on the basis of want, you need to be sure that you not tossing out a potentially good lead. We had a painful experience with this in our own company when our sales force was selling our consulting and speaking services over the phone. One of our tele-sellers was qualifying his leads on the basis of "want" using a couple of questions such as these:

"If there was a program that allowed you to increase your sales without spending a lot of money doing so, would you like to see that program implemented in your organization?"

"Do you ever use professional speakers or trainers in your organization?"

These two particular questions were designed to get a yes or a no. If we get a no to the first question, it means they do not want the benefits of what we have and there is no potential for doing business. A no to the second question means there is a problem with the way our services are provided to the client. We know, however, that the majority of the people we call really want the *benefit* of our program, so in a way we are asking a loaded question. Yet, once in a while, this type of question does flush out those who at least perceive they do not want what we have to offer.

To continue with the painful lesson we learned, we noticed that we were getting a response we had not anticipated getting. Of the small percentage of the people who would be disqualified on the basis of want, we did follow up a little by asking why not. We found out that, in most cases, the reason they did not want us was because they only used in-house trainers and seminar leaders. This response threw us for a loop. At first we could not figure out how to get around this objection, because the prospects had a very definite idea of what they wanted. We decided to take a direct approach and find a way around this roadblock. We called back some of our disqualified leads. This time we probed a little more to find the reason *why* they used only in-house trainers and refused to use outside speakers. We discovered that they felt only someone who was deeply involved with their company could adequately address their particular problems. Furthermore, they did not want to share proprietary information with outsiders, because they feared it might fall into the wrong hands. So, to keep control, they used only in-house trainers.

They were telling us that they only wanted to work with people on an in-depth, long-term basis. That is exactly what we wanted! Once we figured this out, we went to work on a follow-up response to that no. The stumbling block was "in-house." We originally interpreted this to mean someone who was a full-time employee of the company, and, in some cases, that is probably what the prospect meant, too. When we came up with the response, "What do we have to do to become one of your 'in-house' trainers?" that did the trick! By responding to that question, the prospect would explain to us exactly the type of relationship he or she wanted in order to consider using our services. We got more out of the conversation than we bargained for, and the funny thing was that the response was so simple. We got to the point of not only qualifying them on want but getting additional information. As a result, we were in a stronger position to solve the prospect's problems and close the sales later.

Need

Need is very much related to want, but it is also different. Prospects may *want* what you have to offer, but not *need* it for any number of reasons. They may have already bought one from a competitor. Perhaps they have other priorities that they wish to take care of first, even though they would like to have what you are selling. Note that we are talking in terms of the *benefits* of your product or service, rather than the features.

In selling an intangible such as life insurance, for example, you could ask the prospect, "Do you *need* life insurance?" Although this question deals with the prospect's need, it is not a good approach. You are not likely to get a truly accurate response with that question. The prospect may already have some coverage and may not be considering buying more. However, the response would likely be much different if you asked an entirely different question that zeroed in on the benefit. For example: "Is it important for you to know that, should something tragic happen to you, your family would not be forced into poverty?"

Granted, this is an extreme example, but it does illustrate how benefits are what your prospects want and need. Painting these kinds of word pictures in the minds of your prospects helps you convey the real value of what you are offering.

If a stockbroker asks a prospect if he or she is interested in making investments or needs a stockbroker, the response is likely to be negative. The prospect may already have a stock broker or may be working with a financial planner to make investments. Yet, if you were to ask if he or she wanted an investment opportunity that allowed for substantial growth and return on investment with minimal risk, you might find out that he or she wants and needs your services. It all depends on how you phrase the question.

The phrasing of these questions is so important that Bill Bishop, author and producer of the *Million Dollar Presentation* and *Gold Calling*[1] illustrates the point with the story of a young monk.

---

[1]Bill Bishop, Bill Bishop & Associates. 834 Gran Paseo Drive, Orlando, FL, 32825. 407/281-1395. Programs available in audio cassettes and videotapes only.

The young monk had recently joined a monastery and wanted to ask the abbot for permission to smoke his pipe. He approached the abbot and asked, "Can I have permission to smoke my pipe when I pray?"

The abbot responded negatively to the request, and the young monk accepted his decision without question. When the young monk ventured out into the courtyard, however, he noticed an older monk smoking a pipe. Curious now, the young monk approached him and explained that he had asked the abbot if he could smoke *his* pipe when he prayed but had been turned down. Naturally, he wondered how the older monk was able to get permission.

The older monk took a long puff on his pipe and responded, "Well, my brother, when I approached the abbot, I asked him an entirely different question. I asked if it was appropriate to pray while smoking my pipe. He informed me that anytime was appropriate for prayer!"

Decision Maker

The third qualifier is finding out whether you are talking to the decision maker. If you are not, you are wasting your time. If the decision is made by more than one person, then it is vital that you talk to all of the decision makers at the same time. Without talking to the decision maker, you cannot get a yes.

In some instances, you may be forced to deal with a decision influencer, as discussed in Chapter 2. For example, when a client is considering our program for a keynote speaking position for a trade association, the final decision is often made by a board of directors. In most cases, the association's convention coordinator does not let us talk to the board members directly. So, we have to sell our program through the coordinator, who takes it to the board.

Decision Mode

The fourth qualifier is decision mode. Is your prospect in a position to make a decision within a certain time? If you are selling copy machines or FAX machines and your prospect just bought one a year ago, you know that he or she will probably not be in a decision-making mode for at least another year, unless the company is planning an expansion or is not happy with its current equipment. Knowing your prospect's buying cycle is very important.

Budget

The fifth qualifier is money. Is your prospect willing to spend the money for what you are selling? Do *not* confuse willingness to spend the money with affordability. When someone tells you he or she cannot afford something, that is an opinion, not necessarily a statement of fact. The prospect is telling you that you have not been convincing enough to justify the expenditure. Be careful with this one. Often, prospects will tell you that they can spend only a certain amount of money. Yet, if you offer them a terrific opportunity or if they understand the value of what you have to offer them, price will not be much of a problem. But, you will still have a way to go before you reach the close. (In the next chapter, you will learn the StreetSmart Tele-Selling secrets of how to set up the appointment for the next contact. And just as important, you will learn how to reinforce your qualifying call with the proper mail follow-up.)

So, what kind of questions do you ask a prospect to determine if he or she is qualified? Here are some suggestions. For illustration, let's take five different products and services and look at how each one would qualify for each of the five qualifiers.

Let's start with the decision maker. This one is easy, because it is the same question for any business. You do not want to ask, "Are you the decision maker?" because this challenges their egos too much, and you are likely to get a yes when, in fact, they are not.

The question we like to use is: "With whom else would you want to consult before you make your final decision?" See how nonthreatening this is? They may tell you they are the decision makers and would not have to consult anyone else, but many times they actually are not. We like to double check it when they tell us they are.

The follow-up question might be: "That's great. So you're the head person in charge. Wonderful. Let me ask you this. Once you make your decision, whose name actually appears on the contract?" This approach flushes out a lot of gophers and separates them from the real decision makers.

To find out if the prospect needs and wants what you have, you must ask some open-ended questions. We like to start out with something that immediately gets the prospect to do the talking. Questions you might ask to discover wants and needs are ones that tell you whether they are using your type of product or service now or have used it in the past. For life insurance you might ask, "What kind of coverage do you currently have?" The same holds true for investments . . . "What kind of investments are you currently involved in?"

This will start to open some doors. When you start to get this type of information, probe a little deeper to find out why they have what they have. Then find out what they like most about what they have now and what they like least. To do this, ask your questions diplomatically. You do not want to offend them by implying that they made a bad decision.

For instance, you might use the following series of questions with Marc representing an up-and-coming young stockbroker who is qualifying a lead named Mr. Nelson.

"Mr. Nelson, what kinds of investments are you currently involved in . . . stocks, bonds, CDs . . .?"

"Well, mostly CDs and some mutual funds."

"I see. What is it about CDs and mutual funds that you like?"

"With the CDs there's very little risk, so I do not have to worry about the bottom falling out. But, I do like to get a little more return. So I buy into a solid mutual fund once in a while. I like mutual funds because I don't have to watch the stocks every day. Watching them go up and down drives me up a wall, and my doctor wants me to watch my blood pressure . . . you know what I mean?"

"I heard that. So, if I understand you correctly, you want investments that are primarily safe, yet give a decent return. But you like to spice up an investment from time to time with something just a little more aggressive, as long as you do not have to deal with it on a day-to-day basis. Is that a fair assessment?"

"Yep."

"Mr. Nelson, in the past when you have made investments—other than this particular investment that is not performing as well as you'd like—is there anything about dealing with investing that you thought could have been handled better?"

"Yes, Marc, come to think of it. There was a broker I was using before the one I have now who would never return my phone calls. I thought that was very unprofessional and it annoyed me a lot. You know?"

"I understand. It sounds like your broker now is doing a good job for you?"

"He is. Always returns my calls. Doesn't bother me too much with stuff I'm not interested in."

"I see. Let me ask you this. If there was one thing that he is doing now that you could change, what would it be?"

"Well, he is almost too passive. I mean, I'll know about some new investments that are out before he does, and I'm usually the one who has to suggest ideas to him."

"That makes sense. Mr. Nelson . . . let me ask you this. I know you're working with this broker now, and it sounds like he is doing a pretty good job for you. But if I could provide you with some investment opportunities that could potentially boost your return significantly, yet had only moderate risk and were something you wouldn't have to worry about from day to day, would you consider them for part of your portfolio?"

"I don't see why not."

"Super. Let me ask you just a few more questions . . ."

You see, the open-ended questions that Marc asked the prospect opened up a special need and a want, even though the prospect already had someone providing him a similar service. You will notice that it was only after the prospect told Marc what he wanted and what he did not want that Marc knew which way to guide the prospect. He found his "hot buttons." Then Marc asked a "trial closing" question just to see how serious the prospect was: "If I could do this . . . would you do this?"

So, the questions involve: What have you done? What are you doing? Why are you doing it? What do you like about what you are doing? If you could change anything about the way you're doing it, what would it be? Notice that you do *not* ask what the prospect does not like. You will not get the response you want.

Now, let's look at the process of qualifying budget. This qualifier is fairly straightforward. You first figure out, as best you can, into which price level your prospect might fall. You might say something like, "Our clients usually fall into three categories. Some just want to invest a few thousand dollars a year, usually into their IRAs. Then there are the middle-ground investors with $5,000 to

$15,000. And, of course, there are the more aggressive investors who will invest $20,000 or more. In which of these categories do you see yourself?"

The middle category is the one you anticipate your prospect will fall into, but once in a while you might get surprised. Once prospects pick a category, they have told you that they have the money to do it (provided the opportunity warrants the investment). Budget is qualified.

Now you need to qualify on decision mode. You ask, "If there was an investment that you felt was exactly what you wanted, is there any reason that you would not be able to take advantage of it right away?"

Here you are trying to find out if there is anything that could keep you from getting a decision now. Perhaps your prospect has all his or her money tied up into three-year CDs and cannot get it out for another year and a half. That would disqualify your prospect for now, but, of course, you would put that prospect in your tickler file to contact in perhaps a year or so.

With these questions answered, you should now have a good feeling about your prospect. You know he or she wants and needs your product or service. The person you are talking to can make a decision, and he or she has the money and the capacity to spend it now. All the elements are in place. Congratulations, you have gotten yourself a qualified prospect. But do not be a hurry to pat yourself on the back. Qualifying your prospect is very important, but you are far from getting a sale. Later in the book, you will learn how to follow up and move a little closer to getting that commission check.

4

Setting Up the Appointment by Phone

Once your prospect is qualified, you have just begun the selling process. The next phase is critical regardless of whether you want to use the phone to set up an in-person appointment or you want to use the phone for the entire selling process. The purpose of setting up the second contact, whether it is by phone or in person, is to arrange an opportunity to start probing in greater detail to find out the real and perceived needs of your prospect.

The Four Objectives of the Initial Phone Call

STREETSMART TELE-SELLING SECRET #11

You should achieve four objectives in your initial phone call:

1. qualify your prospect,
2. set up an appointment for your next visit (either in person or over the phone),
3. get your prospect to agree to receive and review your mail follow-up, and
4. ask for referrals.

Your first objective, qualifying your prospect, was discussed in depth in Chapter 3. The second objective is to set up a specific time for your next contact. It makes no difference whether you are going to meet your prospect in person or continue to use the telephone for your sales effort. You still must set up a specific time for your next meeting. So, if your next meeting happens to be over the phone, you should still set up the appointment so you have a better chance of connecting with your prospect and avoiding telephone tag.

Setting Up the Appointment

Once you qualify and you have determined that you do want to do business with this prospect, make a suggestion to get together again so you can discuss the business in more detail. You might use something like:

"Well, Mr. Herman, it sounds like we might just have exactly what you're looking for. What I'd like to do first is send some information to give you a better idea of who we are and how we can help you increase your sales. Then, after you have had time to review it, we'll get together again over the phone so we can discuss it in greater detail. I'll be able to answer all of your questions at that time. Okay?"

At this point, you want him to say yes to your question, "Okay?" Once he does, you have his commitment to review the mailer as well as his commitment to set up an appointment to talk again.

First you set up the appointment. You do this by talking out loud to your prospect. It sounds something like this:

"Let's see, Mr. Herman. I can get our information kit out today, which means you'll probably get it on Wednesday or Thursday. You will want a couple of days to review the materials, which puts us at next Tuesday—a week from tomorrow. So I'll get back to you a week from Wednesday. Is that a good day for you?"

If the prospect agrees, the next step is to set up a specific time for the phone call. If it is a bad day, then you obviously must find a good day. So you would continue:

"What's a good time when you could give me 15 to 20 minutes uninterrupted?"

Whatever time your prospect suggests, make the appointment for just a little *after* it, at a slightly odd time. For example, if your prospect says that 10 a.m. is a good time, respond with: "Well, I have 10:10 open. Is that close enough for you?"

By using odd times such as 10, 20, 40, or 50 minutes after the hour, you give your prospects the impression that you are very busy, which you are. They get a sense that your time is very valuable, which it is. Also, it will look peculiar on their appointment books or calendars, and that will keep drawing attention to you. You might even encourage prospects to write the appointment down, to further reinforce it. As an example, you might say:

"Do you have your appointment book handy there? Good, do me a favor and write me down for 10:10 on the 26th, and I'll do the same on my end. Okay?"

Finally, you should close the conversation by reinforcing the appointment time and the arrival of your mailer. And you should ask for recommendations of others who might want your product or service. (Asking for referrals is discussed in more detail later in this chapter.) The total process sounds like this:

"Great. I've got you down for 10:10 a.m. next Wednesday, the 26th. I'll send out the information you requested today. And by the way, if for some reason you need to change our meeting, please give me a call so I could free up that time. Okay?"

"Super. Thanks a lot, Mr. Herman, and I'll be looking forward to talking to you on the 26th. Oh, by the way, who else do you know who could benefit from a program that helps businesses advertise, promote, and increase sales without spending a lot of money? Perhaps another franchisee, supplier, or friend?"

"And why do you recommend them?"

"When I call is there any reason why I shouldn't mention your name?"

"Great. And who else do you know that . . ."

"I really appreciate these referrals, and I promise I'll contact them
     right away. I'll be looking forward to chatting with you on the
     26th. Thanks again. Bye."

Notice that the word *appointment* is not used with the prospect
when referring to the meeting. *Appointment* is a negative word,
usually associated with going to the dentist to get your teeth drilled
or meeting with an IRS agent for an audit. Rather, the very positive
word *meeting* is used. The word *meeting* is even used to describe the
next telephone call. This adds a great deal more importance to future conversations.

Getting a Commitment to Review Your Mailer

The follow-up mailing is important and can accomplish a couple of
things for you, if you can get your prospect to read it. Remember,
most so-called junk mail gets tossed out. But, just as you have
gotten a specific commitment from your prospect to meet with you
for the second time, you should also get a specific commitment
from your prospect to look for and read your follow-up mailer. In
the example of how to set up the appointment, notice how the
prospect has committed to looking for the mail piece. It is no longer
a piece of junk mail, because he will be specifically looking for it.
Unlike junk mail, which gets a readership of maybe 2 to 3 percent,
you can get a readership that reaches toward 100 percent if you use
this approach. The purpose of your first mailer is to reinforce the
benefits you discussed in your telephone conversation. It also helps
build additional credibility for your product or service, for your
company, and, finally, for you—in that order.

Creating the Adver-Teaser

STREETSMART TELE-SELLING SECRET #12

> Never allow your mailers to sell for you. They should only reinforce
> and help you build credibility and rapport with your prospect. All
> selling is done either in person or, preferably, over the phone, so you
> can personally guide your prospect through the buying process.

The goal of the follow-up mailer is primarily to "tease" your prospect. That is why we often refer to the first mailer as an *adver-teaser*. You should not use your literature to "sell" your product or service. Do not give your prospect any nuts-and-bolts information about your program—only the benefits. The reason for this is that once your prospect has enough information, especially pricing information, he or she can make a decision. Without you there to guide them, the only decision your prospect may make is no. Save all of your technical information and prices for the phone call, so you can control the conversation.

The Cover Letter

The first and most important element of your adver-teaser is the cover letter. The cover letter must be a customized letter, written specifically to your prospect. Do not use a preprinted form letter. However, it is perfectly acceptable to use a word-processed letter with the client's name and company name mentioned throughout.

The first sentence of the cover letter should be well written, because it is your headline. It should jump out and capture your prospect's interest so much that he or she wants to read the rest of the letter. Use the word "you" a lot in your letter and stress the benefits.

The following is a letter we use when selling our consulting and speaking services. In this sample, the client is Herman's Hot Dogs, a mythical chain of hot dog stands in and around the Great Neck, NY area.

Date

Mr. Jeff Herman
President & CEO
Herman's Hot Dogs, Inc.
166 Lexington Avenue
New York, NY 10016

Dear Jeff:

It was a pleasure talking with you today about how each of your Herman's Hot Dogs locations can increase sales greatly on a shoestring budget using our effective "Streetfighting" local store marketing program.

As you know, our "Streetfighting" local store marketing program has received a great deal of national attention from publications like the *Wall Street Journal, USA Today,* and *Inc.* magazine, to name a few. This unique program would be developed specifically for your locations.

You will find that our "Streetfighting" program is a welcome addition to your Herman's Hot Dogs marketing efforts, and each of your locations can implement these very effective, easy-to-do sales building programs.

I have enclosed some background material for you that gives you a close view of how our program benefits your operation.

I look forward to talking with you on Wednesday, November 26, at 10:10 a.m., and I will be able to answer all of your questions at that time.

Best wishes,

Jeff Slutsky
President

P.S. John Smith of ABC Company writes, "Your program was very well done and extremely useful."

Notice that the letter gives Mr. Herman absolutely no nuts-and-bolts information, just benefits, credibility, and reinforcement. We want to bring this prospect along slowly, so we begin to build rapport and trust. The more individual contact we have, either by phone or through the mail, the more he feels he really knows us. So we want both frequency of contact as well as quality of contact.

The next critical element of your cover letter is the P.S. It is usually the second thing people read. As soon as they open the letter, they first look for the signature to see who it is from, and then they notice the P.S. So you should always include a post script ("P.S.") in your sales letter. Use a P.S. that grabs attention and causes enough interest to get the reader to go back and read the rest of your letter.

In our example, the P.S. is a quote from a client, yet this quote sells only the benefit, and there is no mention of specifics. Also notice that the word "you" or "your" is used 12 times in the letter. Do not talk in terms of "I do this" or "we do that" but rather in terms of "you get this" or "you are provided with that." Everybody, when presented with an opportunity, wants to know what is in it for them.

Just as powerful is mentioning the client's name several times in the letter. This grabs the reader's attention and is very easy to do on any word processor.

Company Brochure

Other items in your adver-teaser can be any kind of generic promotional material you have around the office. For example, we always enclose our generic brochure, but before we do, we add different color highlighting on key phrases, handwritten notes in the margin directed at the reader, and Post-It™ notes. This technique shows that you have had personal involvement in the piece. By taking your slick, professionally produced brochure and intentionally making it ugly, you will get much more attention from your reader.

Testimonial Letters

You might also include a couple of letters of recommendation from satisfied clients. This is perhaps the only item you will need to go outside your office to get. You will also use more of them later in the selling process, but a couple of strong ones at this point can be helpful. No matter what product or service you sell, testimonial letters are powerful persuaders, especially those that are addressed specifically to you. Remember, you have to sell yourself first, then your company, then your product or service. At this stage, just two letters are enough. Also, remember to take your highlighter and go over the most powerful phrases.

Getting testimonial letters is easy. Just ask. Go to some of your better clients, ones with whom you are on very good terms, and ask them to write you a letter, on their letterhead, that explains how much they appreciate what you did for them. Have them describe the service you personally provided, tell how you helped them to find exactly what they needed, how you got them a good price, and so on.

If they say they are too busy to write the letter, offer to write it for them and have the secretary type it on the client's letterhead. The client only has to review it and sign it. Some of our best testimonial letters are ones we wrote ourselves and got the client to sign!

Publicity

Another item that helps establish credibility is positive publicity you have received. Perhaps your company has been written up in your local newspaper or a trade journal. You might even be fortunate enough to get some national press. These articles should be pasted up on a single sheet of standard paper, if possible, so they are easy to read, with the masthead of the publication at the top. After a year from the publication date, white out the date. This will give you unlimited shelf life. If the publicity is a magazine article, you can create additional impact by having reprints done at your local quick printer on glossy stock instead of using a standard photocopy. This makes the article sharper and crisper, thus creating more impact.

Jeff was fortunate enough to get a major feature story about our Streetfighting program into the *Wall Street Journal*. It was on the front page of the second section, complete with a line drawing of him. We still send out reprints of that article, and it still makes an impact on potential clients, even though it was published on October 23, 1983!

Be sure to white out on your reprints any pricing information or details in the article that might not be current. It is okay to delete information from an article, but *never, never, never,* alter, change, or fabricate information that did not appear in the original. Be honest with your prospect. What may appear to you as an innocent little change in an article could end up destroying your credibility.

How to Get Publicity for Yourself. Publicity about your company or the specific products or services that you sell is important, but publicity about you is very powerful when it comes to building credibility in your information kit.

There are at least two ways to get publicity: (1) by phone; and (2) by mail. Because this book is about using the phone and you are trying to sell yourself to the news media, let's explore the phone option first. Once you have a newsworthy item, you simply contact the appropriate person at the newspaper, magazine, radio, or TV station to inform them of this piece of information. It helps to know who is in charge of specific areas or types of news. To find this out, you need only ask the receptionist who is the business editor or the real estate editor for that publication. Once you have a name, you can call them up with the news item.

When talking to a news editor or reporter, always talk in terms of "your readers," "your viewers," or "your listeners." News people are very sensitive about people looking only for free advertising. You must present your story so that they understand why it would be of interest to their audience. Also, present it in a nonthreatening way. Do not come off sounding like a salesperson.

For example, let's say you have just won an award in your company as the number one sales rep for the entire country. Although this is not necessarily front page news, it could get you a blurb, that is, either a small paragraph or a mention within another story. Almost every hometown newspaper publishes with some regularity a column that mentions the accomplishments of residents. Besides your daily newspaper, there may be a weekly business journal and perhaps a community paper in the area where you work and another where you live. Each of these offers potential for publicity. Also, there are trade journals in your particular industry with circulation on a national, regional, statewide, or even local level. These, too, are good sources of exposure.

Do not forget local TV and radio stations and especially local cable shows that cater to your particular industry. You will find cable shows on topics such as real estate, investments, and business operations. A mention on one of these shows would be helpful. But, of all of the possible publicity outlets, print is the best for building up your information kit. With print, you have the ability to reproduce the item and include it in your kit. With broadcast, this is more difficult.

When calling a reporter, maintain a low-key manner in your voice and use an approach similar to the one that follows: "This is John Smith. I have been a real estate broker here in town for ten years, and this year the American Society of Real Estate Brokers awarded me its silver medal of honor for servicing more than one thousand customers. It's an award that only 1 percent of all registered real estate brokers ever get, and I thought it might be something that your readers might find interesting. What do you think?"

The proposal is simple and straightforward, and at the end you ask for their feedback. If they are interested or not, they will let you know.

The other approach is for a press release. This is a simple, written document that tells all the basics in a simple format. Let's take our fictitious example of Mr. Smith's silver medal and apply it to a press release.

FOR IMMEDIATE RELEASE

For further information contact:

John Smith
John Smith Real Estate Brokerage
1234 Real Estate Way
Brokerage, AK 90012
614/443-5555

John Smith Wins Coveted Silver Medal of Honor

Brokerage, AK—John Smith, president and founder of John Smith Real Estate Brokerage on Real Estate Way, has just been awarded the Silver Medal of Honor by the National Society of Certified Real Estate Brokers. This honor is awarded only to the top 1 percent of all certified real estate brokers who have served 1,000 customers or more. According to Dave Johnson, president-elect of NSCREB, "we are very proud of our winners this year because they represent the elite of their industry and help blaze the way for others to follow in their footsteps."

John Smith started his real estate brokerage company more than 10 years ago, after being a realtor in this area for more than five years. Since that time, John Smith Real Estate Brokerage has grown to become one of the sales leaders in the area and employs more than 25 people. John is married to Susan Smith. They have three children and belong to the Brokerage First Church of God. Smith's hobbies include sailing and collecting beer cans.

Your press release should be double spaced, and all the important information, including who, what, why, where, how, and when, should be answered in the first paragraph. You can add some additional background information if you like, but keep it brief. If a publication or broadcast station wants more information about you, they should know where to contact you.

It also helps to send along a cover letter explaining why you are bringing this information to their attention. After mailing the press release, you might try a follow-up phone call to make sure they have received it and to get their feedback. Also, if the local paper usually prints a photograph, send a good PR photo along. If you do not have one, consider having a professional photographer take one. Do not use a home snapshot.

The quote used in the sample press release is a beneficial touch. Quotes really help add credibility to your press release. Just make sure you quote people accurately.

Another angle that can give you a reason for contacting the news media is to offer helpful "tips" about your field. For instance, if you are a financial planner, tax time is always a good time to show others how to save money on taxes. Whenever there is a change in the tax law is time to contact the media and offer to explain the implications for the average person. Reporters like to quote experts in areas that they are writing about, and once you establish yourself as an expert, you will get plenty of press coverage.

Printing Your Publicity Pieces. Once you have earned some press coverage, you should reproduce it so you can include it in your information kit. And once you have built up your info kit, you may want to have the reprints done on glossy stock, which will give them a richer, more important feel. Adding a second color sometimes lends an additional sense of importance.

When *Entrepreneur* magazine did a review of our book, *StreetSmart Marketing*, we pasted up the review along with the *Entrepreneur* logotype from the title page of the magazine. The combination looked very attractive and professional. Instead of making photocopies, we sent it to our quick printer and had it prepared for offset printing on glossy stock. We had the *Entrepreneur* name printed in red, while the rest of the text and the photo were in black and white. The photograph of the book would not have reproduced well unless the printer sent it out for a velox or PMT. This special photo process enhances photos to make their reproduction of much higher quality. The result of this effort was a great impact for not a lot more money. In fact, when our quick printer came to pick up the order, we asked him if he was going to have red on the press anytime soon. He told us that he was running a job right now in red. So we asked him what kind of deal could he cut if we agreed to turn our print job from a one-color to a two-color run. We got the second color for half price, because the printer did not have to do any special setup with the second color.

Adding a second color to the materials in your information kit is not necessary, but as you progress in your tele-selling career and you begin asking for large sums of money from your clients, you will be helped by anything you can do to show that you represent a quality organization.

The question we often are asked is if the second color and the glossy stock are worth the extra cost. There is no simple answer. Where photocopies may cost you three to four cents each, a two- or three-color printing run on glossy stock might cost you 10 to 15 cents each. That is a significant increase in cost. Then, when you consider that you might put as many as five or six pages of publicity in your info kit, combined with five or six pages of testimonial letters, you have a very significant increase in cost: $.40 versus $1.00 to $1.50. Obviously, this more advanced step is not for everybody, or at least not when you are first starting out. We gradually worked our way up to this over a period of a few years. We started with one testimonial letter from AT&T. It was a great letter with a recognizable logo, so instead of preparing a photocopy, we gave it to our quick printer and had him do it in blue and black on letterhead-quality paper stock. It looked great and added tremendous impact to our info kit. Some prospects would call us thinking they had the original letter! (When there is blue in the letterhead we also have them do the signature in blue, as well.) We got many comments about the letter. Gradually, about once a month, we added another letter in a second color. (A couple needed to be done in three colors.) Each time, we asked our quick printer to call us when he had a certain color on the press for another customer. That way we did not have to pay the setup charge and often got a reasonable deal on the second color run.

But multicolor materials are still expensive, even if you can find a printer offering two colors for the price of one. Here is how we justified the added cost: We figured that the average client we talked to was going to spend an average of $6,000 to $10,000 for a speech or seminar. That is an aggressive fee, but it is what we charge, and what we get. In the mind of the meeting planners who hire us, there is always the concern that they are the only one in the world paying those fees for us and everybody else is getting some kind of deal. The enhanced info kit helps us maintain our fee credibility.

The bottom line for all this, however, is that you should *not* rush into printing these things in two and three colors and on special stocks. Do it when and if it makes sense for you. That often depends on a number of factors, including where you are at in your tele-selling career, as well as how stiff your competition is. If you would like to see our info kit, which includes our brochure, six PR pieces, six letters, and a custom, two-flap folder, send $10 to Info Kit, Retail Marketing Institute, 34 West Whittier St., Columbus, OH 43206. The $10 just barely covers the replacement cost of the kit and the shipping.

Adding Broadcast Materials to Your Info Kit. Turning broadcast publicity into items for your info kit is difficult, as mentioned earlier, but not impossible. One way is to have a photograph taken of you on the TV or at the radio station. With the photo, you can then put together a little flier, almost like a press release, that shows you were on the show. Sometimes the broadcast personality or the show producer will write you a thank-you note for being on the program. That can also be reprinted and added to your kit. If nothing else, you can include the fact that you have been on these various stations when you prepare a biographical sheet on yourself.

Asking for Referrals

That last thing we did in our sample conversation was to ask the prospect for referrals. Conventional wisdom holds that you can get referrals only from satisfied customers. But just think how many referrals you could get from your prospects. After all, you probably have a hundred times as many prospects and dozens of times as many qualified leads as you have satisfied customers.

Just because certain prospects have not bought from you yet does not mean that you cannot ask them for leads. You probably will find that your prospects know other people like themselves who might be in the market for your products and services. So why wait? Ask now. Of course, it is important to ask in just the right way. The question is not "Do you know anyone" but "Whom do you know?" The appropriate responses to those two questions are far different. The first asks for a yes or no answer, whereas the second one asks for the name of a possible referral.

After a name is given you, go on to qualify this lead as much as you can. Asking "Why do you recommend this person?" can give you a little more information and helps you get a clearer picture of the potential prospect even before you make the initial phone call.

Be sure to get permission to use your prospect's name. "When I call Mr. Robinson, is there any reason that I shouldn't mention your name?" It is always prudent to be sure.

Then, when you are done, you repeat the process. "And whom else do you know . . . ?" Do this until the prospect runs out of names. Some prospects may have one or two names, and some may have none. You may even get a prospect with a lot of names. But if you do not ask, you do not get!

Before you are done, thank your prospect for the referral and promise to contact those leads right away. The reason you promise is because, once you begin calling your leads, you can start with: "I promised Mr. Smith I would call you right away." This approach gives a real sense of urgency and importance and helps you get the opportunity to present.

Referrals are much better than cold calls. If you work this part of your tele-selling program properly, you may, after a time, never have to make another cold call again. You could spend all of your time just following up referrals. And you already know that referrals make much better leads than cold calls.

In the next chapter you will get one step closer to closing the sale when you learn the StreetSmart Tele-Selling secrets that help you in your second encounter. This is where you create the perfect state that allows you to get that sale.

5

Call 2—Your Telephone Sales Presentation

Once your prospect is qualified and you feel that he or she is in a position to buy from you, you are ready to make your actual selling presentation. In this chapter, we focus on the importance of the second phone call and the second mail follow-up. The second phone call is where you probe for more detailed information from your prospect and begin to formulate what it is going to take to get the sale. The second mailer, meanwhile, contains all of the paperwork necessary to get the close over the phone during the next call.

STREETSMART TELE-SELLING SECRET #13

> The person asking the questions is in control of the conversation, and you have to be in control of the conversation before you can effectively guide your prospect to a closing point.

The term *selling presentation* is a little misleading, because, even though you are going to inform your prospect about your product or service, you will still communicate in an "investigation" style, that is, you will ask questions rather than answer them. Much of your presentation centers around asking open-ended questions, the way a doctor does when he begins to find out why you are sick or hurting. Only when you have such an understanding, does it make sense to offer a solution, and that solution, we hope, is your product or service.

Being Driven Crazy. Jeff remembers a very unhappy experience when he went shopping for a new car. The odd thing was that after the experience, he discovered he was not alone. Hank Tressler, in his book *No Bull Selling,* recalls a similar experience. At the time, Jeff was driving a big luxury car and thought it was time to buy a sports car. A close friend of his had a very nice sports car and had let him drive it a couple times. Jeff soon decided that the thing he wanted most out of life was to drive fast and look like a big shot.

He started shopping around at a number of dealerships, and every time the same thing happened. Some guy in a plaid polyester sport coat would come out, shake his hand, pop the hood on the car to show him the engine, and then start talking about how much money he could save Jeff. There Jeff was, staring underneath the hoods of these cars. He has no idea how an engine works. He looked at all the tubes, wires, fans, and belts, and it meant absolutely nothing to him. The salesmen kept going on and on about cams and liters and ratios and this and that. Jeff had no idea what they were talking about. All he wanted to do was to drive fast and look like a big shot.

Finally, at one of the places he went to, a salesman came out while Jeff was looking over a particular car. What captured Jeff's attention was that this salesman did not pop the hood. Instead he asked Jeff a question, "I see you're interested in one of our most popular cars. What is it about this car that grabbed your attention?"

He was showing interest in Jeff. And Jeff got a little excited and responded:

"My buddy has one very similar to this, and he let me drive it. I couldn't believe how fast it was and how well it handled."

"You like to drive fast?"

"Oh yeah."

"I had this one out the other day and cranked it up to 140. Is that fast enough for you?"

"Wow!"

"Not only that, whenever I take this car out, everybody thinks I'm a
   big shot."
"I'll take it!"

He had Jeff. He found out Jeff's hot buttons. Jeff had looked at
numerous comparable cars for weeks, but no one had offered the
solution to his problem: to drive fast and look like a big shot. Even
so, the salesman would *not* sell him that car. Jeff could not believe
it. When the salesman told him:

"Listen. You do not want this car, and I will tell you why. For $3,000
   more, I can get you a sticker on the back that says turbo."
"What's it do?" Jeff asked.
"I don't really know, but you can drive faster and you'll be an even
   bigger big shot!"
"I'll take it!"

And he was absolutely right. Everywhere Jeff went, people
noticed the little turbo sticker. He had thought turbo was a type of
fish. But the salesman knew what he wanted to buy and sold it to
him. And Jeff felt great about his decision. He knew that this car,
with turbo, is what he had really wanted all along.

How to Probe for Important Details

Much of what your investigation is going to center around is asking the questions that begin with what, why, how, where, and
who. In your first phone call, you qualified your prospect to make
sure that you would not be wasting your time pursuing a sale that
would never close. Your first follow-up mailer helped reinforce
that first phone conversation and helped build credibility for you,
your company, and finally your product or service. But until this
point, you have given that prospect only a bit of nuts-and-bolts
information.

One of your objectives in the second phone call is to try to
disqualify the prospect. In all likelihood, even though you are using a three-call system, getting the sale will often require you to

make dozens of calls and send out several follow-up mailers. In short, you are going to make a moderate to large investment of time to get each sale. Therefore, if there is a roadblock standing between you and that sale, it is better to find out about it now, during the second phone call, and disqualify the prospect, rather than waste more time and mailers.

Assuming that your prospect survives the disqualifying, your next objective is to dig deep to find out exactly what it is going to take to close this prospect. Although you are not likely to be in a position to close during this second phone call, you can test the waters to get an indication of when you think you can get that decision.

Another goal of the second phone call is to uncover where this sale, once you get it, can lead. You do *not* want to get ahead of yourself. And you always have to assume that at least half of what prospects tell you is either exaggerated or a lie. But you can start to get a feel for the potential. Remember, a sale does not begin and end with this close (if you get it). Instead, find out what kind of continued business you can get and what referral business you can get.

STREETSMART TELE-SELLING SECRET #14

Asking questions, not pitching features, is the way to uncover the real needs and problems of your prospect, which in turn allows you to offer your solutions and close the sale.

Your opening in the second phone call is a quick review of your first conversation. This helps you reinforce important points that you have discovered in your initial phone call to make sure you are both on the same wavelength. On the other hand, you cannot assume anything in the second call. If you use a piece of important information from the first phone call to make a point now, you can get yourself into trouble if your prospect changes his or her mind about that item.

For example, let's say you are selling a photocopy machine. In the first phone call, your prospect told you that his or her firm needs a machine that has automatic feed, collates, and does 200 pages a minute. So you open your second phone call by telling your prospect about the perfect machine that has automatic feed, collates, and does 200 pages a minute . . . and you start going into your pitch on this machine.

Then the prospect interrupts you in the middle of your wonderful pitch and tells you that the boss has decided "we don't need a collator and we have to have a machine that copies in two colors." Your pitch is dead, and you have lost credibility by trying to sell something they cannot use. So, to avoid such surprises, review key points first, so you can made mid-course corrections as necessary.

The brief review follows along the lines of "as you'll recall." Then you get agreement on the key points. For example: "As I recall, John, you need a machine that has an automatic feed, collates, and copies 200 pages a minute. Is that right?" By asking for confirmation, you keep control of the conversation and set the groundwork for your presentation.

Now, let's say the client gives you the new criteria. You can requalify on budget and other items and then go into the presentation about the machine that is most appropriate for your prospect's needs. You also want subtly to double check the prospect's needs. After all, he did change on you once before, so you have to make sure that this is exactly what they need. No surprises.

If you are right, you will have reinforced the prospect's perception of need. If for some reason you are off base, you get an opportunity to make an important mid-course correction before you blow the entire presentation.

After you get agreement on the key points you have just reviewed, you must set the ground rules for the rest of the phone call. Tell your prospect that the purpose of your call today is to provide him or her with more information and background about the product or service that you offer. Then you want to turn it over to the prospect to find out more about his or her interests. Next, based on the conversation, you make a recommendation that the prospect may either approve or (pause as if to search for the right word) *im*prove upon. "Okay?"

With an appropriate response to your question, "Okay?" your prospect knows what to expect, and then he or she has a turn to talk and ask questions. Also, the prospect has agreed to make a decision at the end of the conversation! And if your prospect is not in a position to render a decision, you find that out so you can proceed accordingly.

As mentioned before, the term *presentation* may be a little misleading for the second call, because you are going to listen more than you talk. By this time, you have a feel for what your client wants. Now you play "what if." Once the prospect tells you what he or she wants, you feed it back in the form of a "what if" statement.

For example, the client says, "I need an investment that'll give me a decent return but without a lot of risk." Most salespeople might respond with "Oh great. I have this investment right here that'll do just that." This gives the prospect the opportunity to say, "Okay, let me think about it, and I'll get back to you."

However, if you respond with an "if/then" statement followed by a trial closing question, your prospect is more likely to agree with you. Therefore, you should respond with: "Well John, *if* this program right here could offer you a good return on your investment with minimal risk, *then* would you want to take advantage of it today?"

Asking that question allows you to find out if the prospect is serious or not, because once he or she says yes, your chances of getting the sale, once you satisfy the needs, are much greater.

You might even play with a little more aggressive version of the same game. "Well John, if this program right here offers you a good return on your investment with minimal risk, you would want to take advantage of it . . . wouldn't you?" I have used both and they both seem to work well, so pick the one that feels comfortable to you.

If the prospect buys, then you are home free, but in all likelihood you will find that you are not quite there yet. You need a little more contact. After all, the client has not met you in person yet, and has only talked to you twice on the phone.

Staying in Control with the Echo

One way to stay in control of the conversation and, at the same time, gain a lot of valuable information is to use a technique called the *echo*. We first learned this from Bill Bishop a number of years ago, and it really works great. The idea originally came from psy-chotherapists. If you have ever been to one, you may have noticed that they always answer a question with a question.

"Well, Doc, do you think I'm crazy?"
"Well, Jeff, do *you* think you're crazy?"

This approach keeps them in control and, more importantly, they want you to come up with your own solution. If it is your idea, you are more likely to buy into it.

The same principle applies in sales. Here is how the echo works. You take the last few words of your prospect's comments, and echo them back in the form of a question. So it may sound something like this:

"The problem I have is that I'm not sure how this applies to our situation."
"Your situation?"
"Yeah, you know with the merger going on."
"The merger?"
"Yeah. It's a real mess. This company from overseas is making an offer on the company, and we really don't know where we stand."
"Where you stand?"
"Well, they may want to cut some of the sales force to reduce overhead."

This is a great way to extract information without having to do too much thinking. It gives you the opportunity to figure out the best way to handle the prospect.

As you begin to use the echo technique, you will get a little more comfortable with it. Be warned, however, that if you echo too much, some people start to catch on. After about five or six echoes, they will ask: "What are you, an echo?"

So, alternate it a little by using a few other approaches, too. One that works in much the same way is simply called "Oh?" No matter what the prospect tells you, respond with "oh?" and they will come back with more details. You can use three echoes and an oh, three echoes and an oh, and then, when the conversation is getting really exciting, using a tone of disbelief, you can add, No! You can keep them going for hours, if you want to.

The Second-Call Follow-Up Info Kit

After you have done all of this probing, the next critical element is the mail follow-up to your second phone call. We call this mailer the info kit, and it contains all the necessary paperwork to get the close right on the phone during the next call. By the way, the next call should be made by appointment, set up at the end of the second call.

Even though you must provide your prospect with all the necessary paperwork required to get the order, you do not want to provide *all* the information needed to make a final decision. You should save that for your next telephone conversation.

The paperwork such as contracts, estimate sheets, fee work sheets, and agreements can be handled over the telephone if you use a fill-in-the-blank format. With these types of documents, you can talk your prospect through the agreement. At the same time, you can make your prospect feel more comfortable working with your paperwork, pen in hand, because you are on the line.

The second mail follow-up must be very professional in appearance and content. While your first mailer was just to tease your prospect, this mailer has to help you close your prospect.

Feel free to use again some of the same material contained in your adver-teaser. Repetition of strong elements, such as letters of recommendation and good publicity, helps to establish credibility further. In addition, be sure to include some additional testimonial letters from satisfied customers, which were not in your adver-teaser. This really helps the credibility issue. The same applies to new publicity.

Again, remember to highlight key phrases in both the letters and the publicity. Your cover letter should reinforce the second phone call and will, no doubt, have to be customized for that prospect. But keep it short. This cover letter should not be more than three or four paragraphs if you can help it. The shorter it is, the greater your chances of getting it read. It should serve as a reminder of what to expect with the next call and the third telephone appointment.

Ideally, you should place all of these items in a folder. We like using a folder because it allows us to customize the info kit for each of our prospects. We can mix and match pieces that have the most impact on that client. For example, if we are sending an info kit to a restaurant chain, we would include the articles in *Nation's Restaurant News, Restaurants & Institutions,* and *Independent Restaurant.* On the other hand, if we are talking to a quick-oil-change operation, we would add the articles in *US Oil Week.*

The same holds true for our testimonial letters. When talking to a restaurant chain, we make sure to include letters from Mc-Donald's, Domino's, and the National Restaurant Association. But when sending to a quick-oil-change chain, we include letters from Quaker State Minit-Lube, Jiffy Lube, and Speede Oil. Depending on the type of operation, we might also include a letter from the International Franchise Association.

Make sure that all the contracts and other papers that might scare off a prospect are placed in the back of your folder. You don't want those items to be the first that your prospect sees, although they are necessary when the time is right to close the sale. It helps to put your contracts and order forms in the same position each time, so that when you come to the closing point, you can direct your prospect to the pieces of paper necessary to complete the transaction.

You may not be able to use actual contracts for your fill-in-the-blank process. If not, make up a worksheet that the prospect can write on to determine the final form of the product or service. This worksheet should include spaces to fill in prices. Do not provide a price sheet in writing. Instead, dictate the prices over the phone, so you can be right there to help with the final decision. The worksheets should also include a place for the prospect to sign or initial. Once you get your prospect to sign a worksheet, he has, in his own mind, made the decision to buy. You are not home free yet, but you are very close at this point. The step-by-step procedures of how to do this are covered in the next chapter.

When mailing info kits, especially if they are going out in a folder, consider sending them via UPS (United Parcel Service). We find that they get there faster and often cheaper than using the postal service. UPS is very convenient when you have a rush order in which a prospect needs the information very soon. You have the option to send it second day or next day air, and UPS's air service is very reasonable.

But if for some reason it is absolutely vital that your prospect get the info kit the next morning, use Federal Express. They are more expensive, but in our experience, they have proven absolutely reliable.

The other big advantage of using both these services is that they can track an info kit for you. And, once you establish an account, they will bill you. Try that with the post office.

6

Dealing with Procrastinators and Handling Objections

Dealing with procrastinations and objections is an integral part of the selling process. Procrastinating and making objections are ways your prospect delays making a decision. Your prospect may come up with one objection after another. Some of them may be reasonable and some may be downright crazy. In this chapter, you will learn why people procrastinate and pose objections and how you can get them to make a decision.

STREETSMART TELE-SELLING SECRET #15

Decision making is painful. When people are forced to make a decision, they feel pain and therefore use objections as a way to postpone the pain. A StreetSmart Tele-Seller helps the prospect to make decisions while keeping the pain to a minimum.

Decision making is painful. When you have to make up your mind about something, your brain tells you that you are in pain. Think about the last time you had to make a major decision such as buying a car or a house. It hurt. You racked your brain with objections and procrastinations.

That is a very normal feeling. Bill Bishop, in his audio album *The Million Dollar Close*, describes studies that were conducted to prove this point. Subjects were electronically monitored. During the experiment, the subjects were first pricked with a hat pin. Naturally, they screamed; it hurt. (It is amazing what college kids will do for a few extra bucks.) Their brain waves were monitored on a computer. Later in the experiment, the subjects were forced to make some kind of decision. At this point, the brain waves showed the same response as from physical pain. However, regardless of which decision was made, and whether it was right or wrong, the pain immediately subsided as soon as the decision was made.

The point is that when you ask your customers to make a decision about buying your products or services, keep in mind that they feel pain. When you feel pain, your natural reaction is to do whatever you can to stop the pain. In the case of decision making, prospects may seek to postpone their decisions. They do this with classic procrastination tactics such as, "I want to think about it."

How to Create a Sense of Urgency

With procrastinating prospects, it is important not only to demonstrate the benefits of your product, but also the importance of buying your product now. You must create a sense of urgency to get your procrastinator to a decision-making stage.

Price, availability, and loss of opportunity are perhaps the ideas used most often to create urgency. For example, a real estate opportunity could be lost because somebody else has interest in the same property. That is exactly what happened when Jeff and his wife, Jodi, were buying their first home. They had just started looking and knew they wanted to buy a home sometime in the next six months or so, but they were in no rush. They wanted to find the right house for them and at the right price. They figured they might just stumble onto a bargain.

Lo and behold, a friend of a friend knew about a house not even listed yet. They went to see it, and it was perfect. It needed no work and was underpriced. The owners had bought another house that was costing them a fortune, and they had to get out of the old house. Jeff and Jodi made an offer that night, knowing well and good that they would pay full price on the house, if they had to.

The next morning the owners first showed the house officially. Prior to that, however, the owners had made Jeff and Jodi a counteroffer. They were going to counter again, when Jeff found out, through a very reliable source, that four other contracts were being drawn up—a few at full price. They accepted the owners' counteroffer right on the spot and bought the house.

The owners had created a sense of urgency that forced Jeff and Jodi to act immediately and pay a little more than they thought they had to.

Along the same lines, stock prices can go up at a moment's notice, so your prospect has to act before it is too late. Or, disaster could happen at any moment, leaving your prospect's family unprotected; so it is imperative that the insurance policy get immediate approval. Or, your prospect's business is losing the money and time-saving benefits of not having your computer or telecommunications system installed right now, plus you expect a 10 percent price increase very soon.

So, when you are selling your clients, you are actually selling them on making two different decisions. The first is to buy your products and services. The second is to buy now.

STREETSMART TELE-SELLING SECRET #16

Objections are good. They show that your prospect has interest enough to ask questions.

No matter how good you are at qualifying and bringing your clients along in the selling process, there are bound to be some objections. Some objections will be valid; others will not be so valid, but you will have to deal with them all before you can bring your client to the closing stage.

In this chapter we discuss the real reasons people fire objection after objection at you. And you will learn how to handle those objections effectively and go right from the objection into the close of the sale.

Objections are really good. They show that your prospect has interest enough in what you are offering to ask questions. But, as you have learned many times before, the person who asks the questions controls the conversation.

First, you must determine the level of objection. For example, suppose you are selling a car and your prospect tells you: "I really like it, but do you have it in green?" At this point you do not know if green is a make-it-or-break-it element of the sale. The prospect may just be making conversation. If you do not have it in green, you have opened yourself up to a "well, let me think about it, and I'll get back to you." So when you hear "Do you have it in green?" simply respond with "Do you want it in green?" You may get: "Oh, not really, I was just wondering."

Now, expand that example slightly. Imagine that you know you do not have it in green, but you do not want to open yourself up. If you respond with: "Do you want it in green?" you have given your prospect an opportunity to say "Sure, I'd love it in green." And then you are in trouble.

If you do not have the exact color they have just asked about, you need to find out if that fact can make or break the deal. So you should ask this question: "Is that important to you?" This direct question lets you know exactly where your prospect stands on the issue. For example, your prospect might come back with, "Oh, not real important. Do you have it in red?"

Four Steps to Successful Objection Handling

STREETSMART TELE-SELLING SECRET #17

To handle objections effectively, use the StreetSmart four-step approach:

1. soften,
2. isolate,
3. rephrase, and
4. suggest a solution.

When your prospect starts to come up with objections that sound like she or he is running a little scared, use the four-step approach to objections: soften, isolate, rephrase, and suggest.

Soften

This first step is easy. No matter what your prospect tells you, no matter how crazy the objection is, you simply respond with "I understand." If the prospect says, "I really want it in red," you respond first with "I understand." You see, consumers have been conditioned to be on their guard whenever they talk to anyone who remotely sounds like a salesperson. They know that as soon as they offer an objection, many salespeople try to wear them down to buy. Often there is a big confrontation between the salesperson and the customer.

STREETSMART TELE-SELLING SECRET #18

People do not buy products and services. Rather, they buy solutions to problems.

Such confrontations should never happen. As a professional salesperson, you want to help fill your customers' needs. You see, people do not buy goods and services, but rather they buy solutions to problems. You must function as a problem solver for your customers. Therefore, when they have objections, they put up barriers that you must begin to break down so that you can help them solve their problems.

Even when you probe properly, you will always come up against objections. Your first step is to break down the barriers. By responding first with "I understand," you show empathy. That is why this is called a softener. It helps you get on a special level with your prospects so that there is just a little less resistance when you begin to handle their objections. This, in turn, leads to helping them solve their problems.

Isolate

Your second step is to isolate the objection. Your prospects may have numerous objections subconsciously tucked away that they are saving for the moment when you ask them to make a decision. We are sure you have experienced this phenomenon, and we know how frustrating it is. You may have to spend a lot of time and talent helping the prospect understand that one particular objection is not really a reason not to buy. Then, after you have successfully dealt with that objection, the prospect may come back with "yes, but," and you have to start all over again.

To break the response chain of having to answer one objection after another, isolate the objection by asking a simple question.

"Other than (insert objection), is there any other reason that we can't get the go-ahead with this order right now?"

By isolating the objection, your prospect has told you that this is the *only* reason for not making a decision now. Notice how this technique enables your prospect to agree, and if this one and only objection is dealt with, the prospect gives you the go-ahead.

STREETSMART TELE-SELLING SECRET #19

Avoid painful words, such as "sign" or "contract," that put prospects on alert. Instead, use nonthreatening terminology such as "let's give it the go-ahead, get the ball rolling," or "give it a try."

While dealing with objections, you should avoid using painful words such as "decision," "sign," or "contract." Instead, you should use "go-ahead," "give it a try," or "get the ball rolling." Rather than asking the prospect to sign, you might ask for his "approval." "Contracts" become "the paperwork." These words and phrases are informal and, consequently, make the decision-making process less painful.

STREETSMART TELE-SELLING SECRET #20

In the minds of clients or customers, everything you say is suspect, but they believe that everything they say is the truth, whether it really is or not. Your objective in the selling process is to get prospects to figure out for themselves that your solution to their problems is the best one for them.

A good rule of thumb is to assume that, in your prospect's mind, anything he or she says is true, but anything you say to the prospect is suspect. In order for the prospect to believe what you are saying, you must get the prospect to say it for you. You do this by guiding your prospect along with leading questions in much the same way as a psychologist would help someone with a problem to discover the answer for him- or herself.

The point is that, by asking questions, especially during the objection phase, you not only control the conversation, but you create an atmosphere in which prospects discover for themselves the solution to the problem.

Now, let's tie this back into isolating the objection. By getting the prospect to agree that a particular objection is the only thing standing between you and the sale, it becomes very difficult for that prospect to come back with another objection later.

Rephrase

The next step is to rephrase the objection into a format with which you can deal. For example, if your prospect says, "I cannot afford it," that is a statement. It is very final, and you cannot answer a statement. You can only answer a question, so you have to get the prospect to agree that the statement that was just made was actually a question; then you can offer an answer to that question.

STREETSMART TELE-SELLING SECRET #21

You cannot debate affordability, but you *can* discuss cost and value.

To illustrate, consider this. Your prospect says, "Well, I cannot afford it." You might respond, "I understand . . . so what you are telling me, Mary, is that it costs too much. Is that your question?" Even though she did not ask it as a question, refer to it as if she did. It is very difficult to deal with a question of affordability because what some prospects can afford is often a judgment call. What they are really saying is that they have not yet been convinced that what you have to offer has value enough to justify the expenditure.

Cost, rather than affordability, is an entirely different matter. Cost is not an arbitrary judgment call, but a quantitative amount. Cost is something with which you can deal. Therefore, not only should you convert the objection from a statement to a question, but you should rephrase it so that you can answer.

Let's take another example. Suppose your prospect says, "I do not believe in life insurance." Now you can attack your prospect and try to prove that he or she is wrong. When you attack, keep in mind that psychologists tell us that there are usually only two natural responses: Fight or flight. Either response puts you in a bad position to set up the close of a sale. Psychologists also tell us that there are only four basic emotions: mad, sad, glad, and scared. The only time prospects agree to buy is when they are glad.

Keeping this is mind, simply rephrase the objection as a question. Respond with something like this: "So, if I understand you correctly, Mr. Krel, you think life insurance is not a sound investment. Is that your question?"

Again, notice how we have restated the prospect's statement. It is difficult to deal with what someone believes in. Yet, once Mr. Krel agrees that what he really meant was that he does not think life insurance is a sound investment, you have something you can discuss with him. Furthermore, by tacking on "Is that your question?", you are then given an opportunity to prove why life insurance *is* a sound investment.

Next, you should isolate one more time to make sure you are in a position to close. But before you do, tie in some key information from the initial discovery that was conducted in your first two phone calls.

How to Offer Your Suggested Solution

Let's assume that in those first two phone calls, your prospect's biggest financial concern is putting his two daughters through school. Here is how you respond: "Let me ask you this. If I could prove to you, right here and now, that we have a program available that provides a strong return on your investment and guarantees you that, regardless of what happens to you, your two daughters will be able to go to college, would you give me the go ahead on it?"

Once you get his yes on this hypothetical situation, the prospect has agreed to buy, provided that his specific needs are met. Reaching a specific financial goal is something that every insurance agent is trained to do. So, it is a relatively easy process from here, provided you do not give your prospect any more ammunition to object again.

If you put it all together, the process of coping with objections and procrastinations should flow right along. To illustrate this flow, let's use the example of an advertising media salesperson representing a trade magazine who is calling on a small manufacturer.

PROSPECT: "Well, we really cannot afford to advertise in your magazine right now; Perhaps in the next quarter we might be able to do something."

YOU: "I understand. Other than the cost of the ad, is there anything else that would keep you from placing your ad in the next issue?"

PROSPECT: "No. Not really, but our cash flow is just awful right now, and we just do not want to tie ourselves down at this time."

YOU: "I see. So if I understand you correctly, you really would like to get into our next issue. It is just that you do not have the ready cash. Is that your question?"

PROSPECT: "That's it in a nutshell. Even though this is our busy season for new orders, we do not start getting paid on those for probably . . . oh, 90 days out. That's the one thing I hate about this business."

YOU: "Let me ask you this. How much could you realistically afford, the amount that you would not even have to think about to give me the go ahead?"

PROSPECT: "Gee, I don't know. Maybe about half the budget?"

YOU: "So, if I could show you how to place your ad in time to hit your busy season for half this amount, you'd do it. Is that what I am hearing?"

PROSPECT: "Sure, but how can you do that?"

YOU: "Are you familiar with our special Peak Time Protection Plan?"

PROSPECT: "No, I don't believe so."

YOU: "Well, very simply, it states that we understand your situation, and we can provide a payment program that allows you to advertise when you need to and pay when you get the results."

Of course, if no special credit program were available, then you would have to come up with another strategy to help the prospect understand just how valuable the product or service is. The other option might be to offer a smaller ad that would fit the budget he already told you he *could* afford.

So remember these four steps in dealing with objections. Step one is to soften. No matter what they say, you immediately follow up with "I understand."

Step two is to isolate the objection. You do this by asking, "other than (objection), is there any other reason that we could not get the go ahead right now?"

Step three is to restate the objection as a question that you can answer. "So if I understand you correctly, you think (and you rephrase the objection, then follow it with), is that your question?"

Step four is to suggest a solution in question form. Once the customer has agreed that he or she wants you to answer the question, you can then deal with the one issue preventing you from getting close to the closing point.

Handling the Objection Before It Becomes an Objection

The best way to handle an objection is to deal with it *before* it becomes an objection. Many objections that prospects throw out to salespeople are given to them *by* those salespeople. The problem goes right back to salespeople volunteering too much information, not asking questions, and *not* listening to the customer.

If you get an objection repeatedly, you need to find a way to deal with the objection before it becomes a problem in your sales process. In Chapter 1 of this book, you read a brief story about a successful Midwest sewing machine retailer who used the telephone to generate new customers. Besides getting customers to come in and try out the new computerized machines, he also used the phone another way.

Every year his store offered several classes and seminars on sewing techniques. This not only generated nice revenue for him, but got people to his store, which indirectly created more machine sales as well. His primary medium for filling a seminar or class had been direct mail, but the results had started sagging, so he tried using the phone.

He started initially by calling his customers and conducting a survey to see what types of classes and seminars they would be interested in. When he figured out which would be the most popular, he created a schedule for the classes. Then he started calling once again to fill each of the sessions. At first, he noticed that some people were a little hesitant to commit to a class. This commitment meant giving him credit card orders over the phone to reserve their seats, and they would usually use the objection that they were not available on that date. After a few of these objections, he changed his presentation. Now, when he called, one of the first questions he asked before he got too far into the conversation, was their availability on three particular dates. At that point in the conversation, he was not asking for a commitment, so most of the potential attendees said that they were available. Once they said that they had no schedule conflict, they could not come back later in the presentation and say that they did. This approach alleviated the objection before it became an objection.

This technique is much like the old joke: Just before they go to bed, the husband brings his wife a glass of water and two aspirin. She looks at him and says: "I don't have a headache." That said, there is no way that objection can be used later!

7

Closing the Sale
on the Phone

Nothing really happens until a sale is closed. Everything up to now leads to this closing point, but you can put in a tremendous amount of time getting to this stage of a sale, only to have it fall apart. In this chapter, you will learn several ways to make sure the sale goes through while you are still on the phone. And if you followed all the key points and steps before the close, this is the easiest part of the sale.

Asking for the Order

STREETSMART TELE-SELLING SECRET #22

To close the sale, you have to ask for the order, and you often have to ask for it many times.

One of the first rules of closing the sale is to ask for the order. If you do not ask, you will not get. It is as simple as that! To illustrate this point, consider the following true story: The owner of a rather large printing company was a friend of a bank president, and they played golf together every week for more than 10 years. One day the owner of the printing company said: "Dave, we have been playing golf together for years. How come you never use my printing company?" The bank president responded, "You've never asked me."

One other key point to keep in mind is that it may take numerous attempts at a close before you get a yes. We have read accounts of upwards of seven or more closes before a sale was finally made. Most salespeople quit after just one or two attempts at closing. Yet, if you are persistent and continue to handle all objections, probe deeper, ask more questions, and keep asking for the order, you can dramatically increase your sales production.

Importance of Persistence

The importance of persistence at closing can be compared with the batting average of a major league baseball player. For instance, only a top batter hits in the .300 range. Yet, to bat .300, the baseball player fails to get a hit 7 out of 10 times at bat! Babe Ruth hit more home runs than anybody. He also had the record for the most strikeouts.

The power of persistence was aptly demonstrated early one evening when Jeff was visiting some friends who had a six-year-old boy. Jeff found out that little kids are the best salespeople in the world. The boy ran into the house and asked his mother if he could go out and play with his friends. (The kid asked the question and was in control of the conversation.) The mother responded with no. (She answered a question with a statement. The kid was still in control.) The kid responded with "Why not?" (kid still in control) The mother responded with "Because." (kid still in control) The kid handled objection number three with, "Because why?" Mother responded with objection number four, "Because I said so."

At this point, the six-year-old was asking all the questions and the mother was answering with statements. The kid was in complete control of the conversation. This went on and on until after a dozen or so responses, the mother finally gave in and let the kid go out and play for half an hour. (The kid closed the sale.) The kid then responds with, "One hour?" The mother countered with, "Half an hour! Now get out before I change my mind." The kid left.

Jeff was impressed with this little kid, and his demonstration of basic sales training. He controlled the conversation by using questions. He got the sale through persistence. When the sale was closed, he even tried to suggest a little bigger sale. Classic. Do they come by this naturally or do they learn it? Well, the answer is part yes and part no. Young kids do not have the fear of rejection, so they keep on trying until they get what they want.

Jeff has some further observations on this episode:

"It was not till some time after this experience that I found out why little kids are so good at selling. It is the books they read. After I had my daughter, we picked up a classic book which I started reading to her when she was very young. It was *Green Eggs and Ham* by Dr. Seuss. It is perhaps the best sales training book I have read. The story is based on two main characters. The sales person is Sam I Am, and he is trying to sell The Cat in the Hat on the idea of trying this product called Green Eggs and Ham.

Sam I Am asks choice closing questions that assume the sale.

The Cat in the Hat offers many objections—a pretty tough customer. Sam refuses to give up and repeatedly comes back with other choice closing questions that assume the sale. Finally the Cat in the Hat tells him that he will try it if Sam I Am will agree to just leave him alone. (Of course, he rhymed it a little better than that.) The Cat tries the product and loves it. He thanks Sam for making him aware of this super product, and Sam is now a hero to the customer. Persistence pays off.

When you read this stuff to impressionable five- or six-year-olds, what are they going to think about how to get what they want? Of course, using choice closing questions and assuming a close is an old and overused technique that still works, sometimes. For a five-year-old, on the other hand, it is power stuff. It will probably work for him all the way through junior high school, till he tries using a choice close on a schoolmate. "Would you like to go out with me to a movie or to the dance?" To which she responds: "Neither, you geek."

That is when they start learning about fear of rejection.

The Easy Close

Closing the sale is easy if you set up the close properly. Before your third phone call, you have sent your prospect all the elements necessary to get the sale, including fill-in-the-blank paperwork.

But to get a close, you have to get the prospect to say yes. To get someone to say yes, you have to ask a question that requires a yes or no response as opposed to asking for an opinion. For example, you do not ask "What do you think?" Such a question makes it too easy for the prospect to respond with: "Sounds pretty good, but I want to think about it."

One of the simplest closes that we have seen work is, "I want your business. What do I have to do to get it?" If the response is a reasonable one, do it.

After coming off an objection or even a question, turn it into a close. For example, the prospect might ask, "How long will it take to get delivery?" This red flag tells you that the prospect wants to buy. You lose a great opportunity for a close by saying, "Oh, we can get it to you as early as next week." That allows the prospect to respond with, "Great, I will get back to you." You *must* learn to respond to a question with a question. Let's use that delivery question as our example. Your prospect asks: "How long will it take to get delivery?" You reply: "When would you like to take delivery?" "Can I get it delivered next Tuesday?" Again, do not be too quick to answer the question, because if you answer with something like "Sure, Tuesday is no problem," your prospect can easily come back with "Great, I will let you know."

This process is very much like a verbal chess game in which every move you make depends on the move your prospect makes before you. And, like a good chess player, you need to be thinking three moves ahead.

So, when your prospect comes back with "Can I get delivery on Tuesday?" you respond with, "Would you like delivery on Tuesday?" He might even come back with "What time on Tuesday?" You respond "What is a good time for you?" The prospect might ask, "Can you deliver at 10 a.m.?" You respond with "If I can get it to you at 10, can we put this thing to bed?" Then the prospect might reply, "Sure." And at that point, and only at that point, you come back with the closing remark of "fair enough," and the deal is finally done.

Keep in mind that you never want to let your prospect gain control of the conversation by ending your comments with the answer to a question. Rather, you should follow up with another question to stay in control and bring your prospect to the point where he or she will say yes.

Here is another example of a similar situation. Your prospect asks you, "Does it come in blue?" You respond, "Do you want it in blue?" Another prospect says, "Can I get it with low monthly installments?" And you fire back, "Do you want low monthly installments?", or to gain a little more information on a subject as broad as that, you could respond with, "What type of monthly installments are you looking for?" When your prospect tells you, you can follow up with your "if/then" close, which goes like this . . . .

"If I could get you those monthly installments, could I get your approval right now?"

If the customer says yes, you respond with "fair enough," and the deal is done.

I would caution you to avoid closes that many consumers are already aware of like the famous "Benjamin Franklin" close or the "choice" close. The choice close is, "Would you like it in green or red?" And, of course, no matter which one they choose, you have a sale. "Did you want to buy the large one or the extra large one?" "Did you want the plain or the peanut?"

Consumers are wise to this, and it is easy for them to come back with neither choice and say, "Let me think about it."

The Last-Ditch Effort

One of our favorite closing techniques is one that is used when you are absolutely sure the sale will not get closed. At that point, after perhaps seven different attempts at getting the client to commit to using our company, the salesperson takes a deep breath and asks in a somewhat confused manner, "Can I ask you just one final question, then I will let you go?"

At that point prospects' defenses drop completely because they know we have finally accepted their decision not to buy from us. So, they usually agree.

Then the salesperson responds:

"It is obvious that we are not going to be able to get together here, so it would help me out tremendously if you could give me an answer . . . What did I do wrong?"

"Do wrong?"

"Well, obviously I could not convince you that what we had was what you needed, so I did not do my job right; and for that I am sorry. But I really would like to know, to help me in the future, just what I did wrong?"

"Well, Jeff, I don't think you did anything wrong. I just don't think that your program is right for us because . . . ."

At that point, the prospects go on to tell you exactly why they did not buy from you and exactly what it would take to get them to buy from you. It is at that point that you would continue with your presentation and go right for the close addressing those issues.

This technique takes what otherwise would have been a dead issue and not only brings it back to life, but puts you in a position really to turn it around.

STREETSMART TELE-SELLING SECRET #23

Admitting a mistake and learning from that mistake is the key character trait of a successful tele-seller.

Salespeople's egos kill more sales than anything else. Many times we have seen a salesperson refuse to admit making a mistake or not knowing the answer to every question a customer might have. Many of us are driven both by ego and by greed, but you would be surprised that ego usually outweighs greed when it comes to the driving force behind many successful salespeople.

Because of their egos, many salespeople cannot admit a mistake. They have to be right all the time. But knowing when you are right *and* wrong is the difference between a mediocre salesperson and a super salesperson.

The reason we bring this up is that you often have the best closes when you admit to making a mistake, whether you really did or not. This brings down much of the wall that the prospect put up and allows you to develop rapport.

There are a number of fine books and tape programs available that illustrate various types of closes, and you no doubt have some closes that work for you. Some programs we encourage you to study include:

Successful Telemarketing in the 80's by Martin Shafiroff and Robert Shook; George Walther's tape album, *Effective Telemarketing* and his book *Phone Power;* Dorothy Leeds' book and tape on *Smart Questions;* Bill Bishop's tape programs entitled *Gold Calling* and *The Million Dollar Close;* Stan Billue's audio and video programs; and *No Bull Selling* by Hank Tressler. (See the *Streetfighter's Resource Guide* for details on each of these programs, including ordering information.)

Up-Selling at the Post-Close

STREETSMART TELE-SELLING SECRET #24

The time to increase your sales is immediately after you have closed the deal. Have some post-closing, up-selling products or services that you can suggest just after the close that increase your sale by 10 to 30 percent.

Another area of closing is actually the part of the sale immediately after the close. This post-close is where you do your up-selling. It is much easier to get more business from an existing customer than from a new customer. And the easiest time to get your customers to buy more is when they have just bought.

To illustrate your up-selling opportunities, imagine drawing a wheel on a piece of paper, with many spokes extending outward from a small circle in the center. In that circle, in the center of the wheel, you see the words "product or service bought." (See Figure 7-1.) From the center, the spokes extend outward, with each spoke representing a different product or service you offer. This serves as a constant reminder not only that you need to close the sale, but once you have closed it, to build on it.

The first sample up-sell wheel is the one my staff uses. Because we are selling speaking and consulting services, we have all of the various products and services represented.

When a client agrees to use us, let's say for a half-day seminar, we can then, using a little more probing, find out if it would better suit his or her program and still be in the budget to consider a

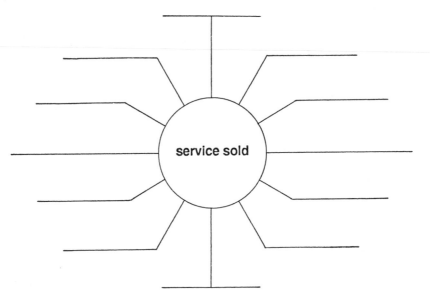

Figure 7-1 Example up-sell wheel for consulting and seminar firm.

keynote speech the night before. How about having workbooks for each of the participants or perhaps both workbooks and copies of our book? Would they like to buy the rights to record the seminar or perhaps have us do a few months of consulting so that their program can be customized more specifically?

Of course, if the client wants only the $3,000 program, that is what he gets; but we offer and suggest other possibilities to the client.

For insurance, you might put all the various types of policies and options on the spokes of your wheel. The time to sell your client an extra $10,000 of coverage is just after he or she bought $100,000 worth. It is easy to suggest politely, "You know, Tom, you just bought a great policy here that gives you $100,000 of coverage. We have a special program going on that allows you to increase your coverage by 10 percent for just a few dollars more a month. Would you like me to put it down for you?"

More often than not, they respond with, "Sure, go ahead."

That extra 10 percent is no big deal to your client; for you, 10 of those is like getting a free customer.

One of the more interesting up-sell approaches for insurance was used by a property and casualty agency that would package a life insurance policy into its program. They already had the credibility and rapport with the client, so it was easy to suggest including that small life policy with the package with a "by the way, as a special arrangement with our clients, we offer the following option . . . ."

An up-sell wheel could be made, for example, if you are selling a photocopy machine. You could sell all kinds of extras, such as a stand for the machine, a collator, automatic feed, extra supplies, a service contract, or special financing, perhaps even a FAX machine.

Make an up-sell wheel to suit your needs, so that no matter what you put in the center as the product or service, you can go around the wheel and think of new combinations and packages to offer your clients. That way, you can serve them better and at the same time increase the amount of your sales. Everybody wins.

Closing over the phone requires not only good basic closing techniques but some special techniques, as well. To help you, the remainder of this section focuses on those special techniques.

Getting the Paperwork Ready

STREETSMART TELE-SELLING SECRET #25

To close a sale on the phone, you have to have all the necessary paperwork in the hands of the prospect, preferably in fill-in-the-blank form.

The key difference between closing in person and closing over the phone is that closing over the phone does not enable you to hand your prospect a pen and get him or her to sign the paper. So you have to be a little creative.

We discussed briefly the need to use fill-in-the-blank forms. These are very important. It can be the contract, order form, worksheet, or other document that forces the prospect, while on the phone, to pay attention and follow some simple directions.

Some of the fill-in-the-blank tasks are done during the presentation stage; for example, a worksheet that allows prospects to figure out costs based on different options available. For that reason, it is not a good idea to provide clients with a published price

STREETFIGHTING SPEAKING AGREEMENT

This SEMINAR AGREEMENT is executed on _____, 1989 between Retail Marketing Institute, Inc. (INSTITUTE) and _____(CLIENT).

     In consideration of the institute presenting a Streetfighting marketing program at CLIENT's request, the INSTITUTE and CLIENT agree to be legally bound as follows:

I. ENGAGEMENT OF INSTITUTE:

(a) The CLIENT employs the institute for the program(s) listed below to be presented by _____

(b) The INSTITUTE accepts the employment for program(s) and materials listed below:

Presentation(s)	Length	Location(s)	Date(s)	Fee

Materials Ordered		Quantity	Unit Cost	Total

II. COMPENSATION OF INSTITUTE:

(a) SPEAKING AND MATERIALS FEES -- The CLIENT agrees to pay the INSTITUTE a total fee of $_____(US). CLIENT agrees to return all unused, undamaged, non-customized materials at CLIENT expense within seven (7) days following presentation and pay 5% restocking fee. CLIENT further agrees to pay late fees for materials not returned equal to 10% of the value listed above for each additional seven (7) day period, to fee to exceed total value listed.

(b) DEPOSIT & CANCELLATION -- A non-refundable deposit of one-third of the total fee, within seven (7) days of this signed agreement is required to reserve your date. Deposit is forfeited in the event of cancellation or postponement. If program is cancelled within 90 or less days prior to reserved date, CLIENT agrees to pay the full fee, due by the presentation date. All cancellations and postponements to be handled in writing.

(c) 10% PRE-PAY DISCOUNT OPTION -- CLIENT has the option to receive a 10% discount on entire speaking fee When date(s) are reserved with payment in full and receipt of the this agreement. In the event of cancellation 90 or more days prior to the scheduled presentation, one-third of the non-discounted fee is forfeited.

(d) EXPENSES -- All expenses are included in the speaking fee when conducted in the Continental United States. Does not include optional materials.

(e) CONTINUING EDUCATION -- INSTITUTE agrees to make available to CLIENT's attendees, for sale at a discount, the Streetfighter's Profit Package audio/video training program.

(f) RECORDING FEES & CONDITIONS -- CLIENT has the option to buy the rights to record by audio and/or video, all or part of the presentation with an additional fee equal to 100% of the speaking fee. INSTITUTE is to be provided one high qualify copy of the recording(s) within fourteen (14) days following the presentation to be used at INSTITUTE's discretion. Otherwise, CLIENT agrees not to record, or allow to be recorded by members of the audience, any portion of the presentation without buying the recording rights.

III. GOVERNING LAW:

This agreement shall be governed by and construed under the laws of the State of Ohio.

The INSTITUTE and the CLIENT, being sole parties to this agreement, sign this agreement.

_____Date_____   _____Date_____
Retail Marketing Institute, Inc.   _____(CLIENT)
Jeffrey L. Slutsky, President   _____(name, title)

Figure 7-2   Fill-in-the-blank agreement for closing the sale over the phone.

sheet, even if your prices are fairly steady. Instead, provide prospects with sheets that list the types of goods and services you have available and have blanks to be filled in with prices. Then talk prospects through the price sheets and get them to update the forms as your talk. This requires your prospects to get involved in the conversation and keeps them from being in a position to make a decision until you are together on the phone.

You make this work by having duplicate sets of the materials you sent your prospects. Here is how the process might go:

"Okay, Bob, you have the Streetfighter's worksheet and the investment schedule in front of you. Do you have your calculator handy?"

"All set, Marc."

"Great. The first thing we do to kick off your program is the full-day seminar with an assistant. So, put $5,750 in the first blank next to seminar. Okay?"

"Got it."

"Next, you need one field day for every four stores we'll be working with. How many stores do you want in this program?"

"Well, there are at least 11 stores that I'd like to have participate."

"No problem. You might as well add one more because the investment is the same, so let's put 12 stores down on the second line, which is a total of three field days and multiply that by $750 per field day. What do you get there, Bob?"

"I get $2,250."

"Same here. Put that on the field day line. Next, we need to figure out the office support days, which are the same as the field days, so we put $2,250 there. And when we add up the total days, both in the field and in the office, we get $4,500, right?"

"Yep."

"Now, all we do is figure out the total by multiplying the monthly investment by the total months of the program, which is 12. What do you get, Bob?"

"Let's see. Twelve times $4,500 is $54,000."

"Then just add the initial seminar of $5,750 to that and we get?"

"I get $59,750."

"Yep, I get the same. So when you figure in expenses over the 12 months, we come in way under the $75,000 budget figure you had to work with. Right?"

"Sure enough."

"Great. All I need for you to do now is autograph the bottom of that worksheet and FAX it to me. With that, I can get the ball rolling now. Then just pop the original in the mail to me, and we can work out all the other paperwork later. Fair enough?"

"Sounds good to me. Let's do it."

You can use this technique in your second phone call to get your prospect used to working with you in this manner. Then, in your closing phone call, which is the third call at the earliest and more than likely a dozen calls later, you can use the same technique to get the final paperwork done.

Now, to make sure we have our prospect committed to buy from us, we like to have them FAX the paperwork to us. Your legal department may not accept a FAX copy as a legal document, but the reason we want it is to know that we have the commitment. We then have them mail us the originals. Once we see that signature on the FAX copy, we feel much stronger that the deal is made—not 100 percent, but close.

If you do not have a FAX machine, consider getting one.

Fax Cover Sheet Alternative

When faxing, instead of using the normal fax cover sheet, we prefer to use a regular business-style letter. We then leave room at the top of the letterhead for a Post-It™ brand FAX transmittal memo 7671. It is 4" by 1 1/2" and provides boxes to fill in for all of the pertinent information (i.e., to, from, company, department, FAX numbers, number of pages). Then, if you want to follow up with the original letter in the mail, you do not have to do double duty.

With or without a FAX, you do need to get the signed paperwork as quickly as possible. In the information kit, we put a Federal Express Next Day Letter envelope along with an air bill completely filled out. The 9 by 12 shipping envelope is folded in half and placed in the back of the folder. When we get prospects to sign the paper, we tell them to put it into the Federal Express envelope we have provided. Then *we* call Federal Express to pick it up. We leave

Post-It™ brand fax transmittal memo 7671	# of pages ▶	
To	From	
Co.	Co.	
Dept.	Phone #	
Fax #	Fax #	

Figure 7-3   Fax transmittal memo. Just stick it at the top of your cover letter or memo.

very little up to the prospects. Remember, they have a lot on their minds and a lot to do. Your order may not be their priority. Leave nothing to chance.

At the point at which prospects have agreed to buy, don't forget to look at your up-sell wheel or whatever device you use. Suggest at least one more product or service enhancement that makes the purchase that much better for them, and gives you a little more commission.

Closing the sale is what it is all about. You have just learned some simple ways to apply most of the closing techniques you already know to getting that sale on the phone.

In the next chapter, you will learn how you and your company can provide service over the phone so that your customer becomes a long-term client who continues to buy from you for years to come.

8

Servicing Your Customer
Using the Telephone

STREETSMART TELE-SELLING SECRET #26

**It is easier to get repeat business and referral business than it is to get
new customers, so use the phone to service your existing customers
and keep them happy with you, your product, and your company.**

Servicing your clients after the sale is just as important as
selling them, perhaps even more so, because getting more business
and referral business from a satisfied client is much easier than
getting a new customer.

Good service is costly. But, when you learn how to service via
the telephone, you can help your clients with their problems and
afford to keep in regular contact with them, as well.

We are already starting to see more and more servicing and
training over the phone, particularly in the computer software field.
Telephone support is valuable and affordable. A training or service
person coming on premises would cost a prospect a fortune, and he
or she would probably be less likely to call that person in with a
simple problem, even though it is costing money and valuable time.

Doctors and lawyers are finding out just how profitable telephone advice is. For what they used to give away, they now
charge—and rightfully so. After all, what is the difference between seeing a doctor or a lawyer about a relatively easy matter in

person or talking to him or her on the phone? You get the same information, and it allows you to take care of your problem. Yet, both you and your professional spend less time and money doing it. Everybody wins.

For most of us in sales, however, servicing the client over the phone requires some extra skills. You not only have to understand how to fix the problem yourself, but you have to be able to explain the situation clearly enough to the client that he or she can carry out your instructions.

You have probably heard of instances in which someone defuses a bomb using instructions received by telephone or radio, and, of course there occasionally are dramatic accounts of an untrained passenger who lands a plane solely by oral instructions after the pilot has gotten ill or died. The point is, *you* can provide service and training over the telephone, too.

Some companies are finding that service by phone is rapidly becoming a profit center and slowly but surely people are becoming willing to pay for advice and training over the phone.

STREETSMART TELE-SELLING SECRET #27

Providing service over the phone saves your customers time and money while involving them in your product or service.

The telephone can be a key tool for providing service to your customers. With the cost of service calls increasing, it makes sense to look at your phone, not just as a means to cut costs, but to provide faster service.

In this chapter, we present some secrets on how to service your clients successfully by means of the telephone, thus saving both you and your clients time and money.

Advantages of Service Over the Phone

When a computer or copy machine goes down, it is to the customer's advantage to work with a technician via the phone to solve the problem. If it would take a couple of hours or a couple of days to get the repair person there, the customer might be more than willing to invest in a 20-minute phone call first to try to get the machine up and running again. Even if the problem cannot be completely corrected via the phone, at the very least, a diagnosis can be made so the repair person can bring the right parts and equipment to fix the machine during the initial service call. Thus, multiple service calls can be eliminated.

Service by phone can be a great selling tool for you. If your service department helps customers immediately over the phone, this is an excellent benefit that can lead to an effective close in your selling.

Sometimes it is just not possible to send a repair person out, and telecommunication is the only way you can repair something. Consider the plight of the astronauts on Apollo 13, the ill-fated third manned mission to the moon. An explosion in the service module of the space capsule threatened the lives of the three space travelers. There was no way NASA could send up a couple of repair people to fix the problem, since Apollo 13 was halfway to the moon at the time.

By working with technicians on the ground, in conjunction with the three astronauts in the space capsule, NASA was able to improvise devices and repair enough of the equipment to bring the crew home safely. It is amazing what can be done via the telephone.

Remember that it is one thing to win over a customer—but quite another to keep his or her business on the books. So, once you have won the initial order, you must provide outstanding service to get repeat business. In many cases, the original order is minute compared with the potential future business that is generated by a satisfied customer.

Sometimes long-term sales relationships are simply a matter of communicating with your customer—staying in touch with them so they know you truly care about their welfare. Again, periodic telephone calls are the most cost-effective method to let them know that you have their interests at heart. "Hello, John, it's me, Tom. I just called today to see if there is anything I could do for you? Also, as long as I have you on the line, let me explain to you a new service my company now offers . . . ."

When you communicate frequently with your customer, it is very difficult for a competitor to come in and take away your business. This personal touch creates a customer loyalty and a special relationship—the kind that can last for a lifetime.

According to Robert L. Shook, author of *The Perfect Sales Presentation* and co-author of *Successful Telephone Selling in the 90's,* within two years after entering the sales field, if you service your customers properly, an estimated 80 percent of your new sales will either be from satisfied customers or their referrals, or both. So, do not be like those short-sighted salespersons with dollar signs in their eyes who are so busy seeking new business that they fail to service their existing customers. If you are in the sales field for the long haul, it is simply good business to give good service. And, whenever possible, we recommend you do it via the telephone.

Servicing the customer by phone does require special verbal skills. You must be able to paint a clear picture in the mind of the person receiving service. This communication allows the customer to be your hands and eyes for that particular predicament.

If you are helping the customer fix a piece of equipment, you should have a duplicate piece of equipment right in front of you. This can help you explain to that person exactly what you are doing to fix the problem.

Second, have a checklist in front of you to guide the person through, so you are sure the problem is not some simple oversight. One time we were having trouble getting our computer's printer to work. It was getting power, but it would not print out. It just stopped in mid-sentence and refused to go another letter. We tried everything, including re-booting the computer, turning the power off and on, using different diskettes for the word processing program, and so forth. Nothing worked.

Finally, we called the computer support number and explained the problem. The first thing the service person asked was, "Is it plugged in?"

At first the question seemed almost insulting. But when we looked behind the computer, sure enough, the patch cord from the computer to the printer had come unplugged.

It was amazing how well it worked once everything was hooked up again.

Telephone Service Tips

As you get calls for certain problems, be sure to log those problems and what it took to fix them. It is very likely that someone else will have the same problem, and when it occurs again, you will be prepared.

Record your conversations. This allows you to review for yourself just how well you did in guiding the person along. Listen to the words you used to describe certain situations or operations of the equipment. Then ask yourself, "What words, phrases, or examples could I use that would make my explanations more clear next time, should a similar situation arise?"

Get constant feedback. Do this by asking open-ended questions. If you give an involved instruction or description, it is best not to ask a yes or no question but rather ask a more open-ended question that brings more information. For example, instead of asking, "Does the copy you get seem to be too light?" you would get more information by saying, "Describe to me how the copy looks." You may get different information that will help you fix the problem sooner.

With each service success story, get the customer to write you a thank-you note. You can do this with a follow-up survey by suggesting that the customer write you a letter. Or, when they are thanking you over the phone for making their life easier, ask:

"Would you put that in a brief letter? It would help me out a lot." Many people will. Those letters are great for boosting your credibility when the success of a future sale depends on your ability to prove how good you are at support.

When giving advice over the phone, as in the case of a lawyer, consultant, accountant, and the like, it is sometimes best to provide written follow-up to your conversation. This can be a brief note, a memo, or a full report.

Time your phone service conversations. See how long it takes, on average, to help each client. You want to know how many people you are helping and how long it takes each one. This gives you an idea of the kind of expansion you might need when your company grows. The time records are also one way to judge the improvement you are making in helping clients over the phone. As long as your success ratio of fixing the problem is constant, but the amount of the time it takes for you to fix it drops, you are improving. You may want to use a device called a phone accountant to track your phone calls. We describe that device later in this book.

When giving word cues to help someone find certain parts of equipment, use a few different types of descriptions, because different people respond to different cues. For example, if you instruct someone to find a switch, give its size, shape, color, and position, as well as anything that makes it easier to locate. Remember to incorporate all of the senses—sight, hearing, touch, smell, and taste—when appropriate.

What are the opportunities in your company for telephone servicing? Of course, you need to figure out how you can apply these ideas for the sales service you personally provide your customers and to consider all the technical and repair support your company provides. Though it may be out of your area, you can suggest ways the service department can offer an increased level of support to your customers, using the phone. After all, they are *your* customers, too. The better the service department is at taking care of them, the more sales you will make.

Calling Old Customers

One of our first exposures to servicing over the phone was in a local store marketing project for a small quick-print chain several years ago. We noticed one day that the owner had one of his people on the phone calling old customers. She was working from a computer printout sheet and was calling all the accounts that had been inactive for six months or more.

When she called, she simply introduced herself and mentioned she had noticed that the customer had not been in to see them for a while and wondered if there was anything that the company had done that they were not happy with. In many cases, there might have been a small problem with an order, and the customer decided to go elsewhere. These are the most dangerous situations, because you are not aware that a customer is dissatisfied. For every complaint you get, there are perhaps dozens you do not get. If you do not know anything about it, there is little you can do to rectify the situation.

According to Dr. Michael LeBoeuf, Ph.D., author of *How to Win Customers and Keep Them for Life,* [1] most dissatisfied customers

---

[1]Dr. Michael LeBeouf PhD., *How To Win Customers And Keep Them For Life,* Putnum. Also available as a six-audio-cassette album (Nightingale Conant Corporation, 7300 Lehigh Road, Chicago, IL).

simply do not say a thing and vow never to return to your business or use your products or services. Furthermore, they are likely to tell many of their friends and associates about their negative experience with you. On the other hand, if you solve the customer's problem on the first try, there is a very high percentage that that customer will remain your customer.

Of those customers that the quick printer's representative reached who were unhappy with something the printer did, she was able to get close to half of them back. She offered to do the job over or give them a complete credit for the job, and that brought many of them back for another try.

In some cases, she found out that another quick printer had opened close to the customer or the customer had moved to a location less convenient to the printer. For those cases in which a customer had switched to a competitor, the phone call was often all it took to remind the customer of the firm. This particular printer had an impeccable reputation for service—anything to make the client happy. They were not the cheapest, but they provided good quality and good service. As a result, many customers were spoiled. So the phone call jarred their memories and they realized they missed that great service and some of them came back for that reason.

The point is that the phone can be a wonderful marketing tool for reaching customers and clients who are inactive. They do need to be reminded from time to time.

We had a similar experience after we had done a great deal of work for a Chicago-based property management company. About a year had passed since we did the job. One day we called the client because a national association in the property management area was considering bringing us in to keynote their convention. We thought it would help the sale to have a letter of recommendation from the client. (We practice what we preach.)

After talking to the client briefly, they were happy to send us a letter and even offered to call the association for us to give us a plug. Not only that, but the client, prompted by our phone call, remembered they had a property that needed some help, and we were just the guys to do the job. So, here was a case of getting business from an old customer, and the phone call we made had been about something else entirely.

The lesson to be learned here is to go back through your old customer list periodically and give those people a call. You may find that there is a very good reason they stopped buying your products and services. Then again, you may find yourself in a position to get more sales from old clients.

It can help if you institute a system that provides some kind of warning when a customer is in danger of becoming a former customer. George Walther, author of *Phone Power*,[2] compares a telemarketing and sales effort to that of putting and keeping a customer on a conveyer belt. The most important part of your job is to *keep* the customer on the conveyer belt, because you will make much more profit from the sales you get from existing customers than you will from the initial orders of new customers.

Develop a "red flag" system. You need to know what each customer's regular buying cycle is. If he or she usually orders from you monthly, and you do not get an order for two months, you need to know. If you let the lapse go on too long and there is a solvable problem, it may become too late to do anything about it.

By the same token, it is not always necessary to wait for customers to stop buying to find out how they feel. Call them up once in a while to see how things are going. But really dig. Try to flush out small problems now before they become large ones. Use open-ended questions instead of yes or no type questions. If you ask a customer something like "How are things going?" or "Are you happy with what we're doing for you?" you are likely to get a positive response regardless of the situation. The fact is that most people do not like to make waves.

On the other hand, you should ask the customer: "If there is one thing that we're doing that you think we could do better, what would it be?" Does this question sound familiar? It should. A similar one was used when originally qualifying the client. The way this question is stated makes it very easy for the customer to offer suggestions on ways to improve. You are specifically asking for suggestions, and you are likely to get a real response.

We use this question a lot when trying to determine just how we really did after a speech. Many times clients tell you that they liked it and you are basking in the glory of getting a good response from the audience. Yet, this kind of feedback, although great for

---

[2]George Walther, *Phone Power*. Also available as six-cassette album through Nightingale Conant, Chicago, IL.

the ego, does not help you improve. We start asking the question, usually in a follow-up phone call after the presentation, "If we could change one thing about our program to make it a little better, what would it be?" As a result, we have received some wonderful feedback that we would not have gotten otherwise. It has allowed us to constantly improve our programs and help our clients get more value.

The question is a scary one, no doubt. We have all had people advise us, "let a sleeping dog lie" or "if it ain't broke, don't fix it." In sales and customer service, however, these idioms just do not make it. We refer to these sayings as "idiot-oms." The ostrich approach to dealing with potential problems—sticking your head in the sand—only makes it easier for your competition to come along and kick you in the rear end!

9

Doubling Your Tele-Selling Results

The only time you are making money is when you are on the phone selling. Use your primary calling time for selling and do all other tasks in nonprime selling time.

Regardless of the level of your sales skills, selling is a numbers game. Selling by telephone is even more so. The more calls you make, the more sales you get. Therefore, to get the maximum number of appointments or orders from your StreetSmart Tele-Selling efforts, you must look for every possible way to make the best use of your prime telephone calling time. This, in turn, allows you to make the most money you can. Remember: *The only time you are making money is when you are on the phone selling!* You do not make money doing paperwork, filling orders, filing reports, running errands, or looking for leads.

Once you have a program put together to help you make money by selling on the phone, we can show you how to make even more money by making better use of your time. In this chapter we explain ways you can double, or even triple, your productive selling time on the phone.

STREETSMART TELE-SELLING SECRET #29

> Accurately tracking the results of your telephone selling activities helps you make improvements in all aspects of your tele-selling.

Lesson number one for increasing your sales by telephone is: Do not waste valuable telephone selling time doing tasks that could have been done at another time or better yet, by someone else. If you are selling business services, for example, your peak selling hours are between 9 A.M. and 5 P.M., so you want to spend as much of that time as possible on the phone. Selling life insurance to married couples may mean that your prime selling time is in the evening when most people are home from work, from 6 to 9 P.M.—or perhaps on weekends. So the first thing you must do is figure out when *your* prime selling time is. How many total hours do you have in a given day or week to actually make calls?

By tracking your calling efforts, you may also discover that, even though theoretically your prime calling time is from 9 to 5 Monday through Friday, not all days are created equal when it comes to getting through to your prospects. You may find through this tracking that Monday morning before lunch and Friday afternoons after lunch yield much less results than all the other available days and parts of days. Thus, you may need to define your prime calling time as Mondays, 1 to 5; Tuesday through Thursday, 9 to 5; and Fridays 9 to noon.

Also keep in mind that when there is a three-day weekend because of a national holiday, the Thursday afternoon before that Friday off or the Tuesday morning following a Monday off might be just as weak.

The reason you need to be aware of these factors is that you have only a certain number of hours during the day when you can effectively sell. If you have to run an errand or do research, you want to avoid doing that during your prime calling times.

If you know that certain times on certain days are strong for getting sales, you want to make sure you do not plan any other nonselling tasks then. Schedule nonselling tasks for a less valuable time slot instead.

Be smart with your time. If it takes an hour a day for you to get organized, be at your office at 8 A.M. or stay late—but do not waste your valuable selling time on research.

	MON	TUE	WED	THU	FRI	SAT	SUN
8:00							
9:00							
10:00							
11:00							
12:00							
1:00							
2:00							
3:00							
4:00							
5:00							
6:00							
7:00							
8:00							

Figure 9-1   Charting your prime calling time tells you a lot about the effective use of your selling time.

Do you know what your selling time is worth to you? Figure it out. Take the money you made last year and divide it by the actual number of available selling hours you worked that year. These are not the total hours you spent on the job, but only the time you spent presenting to a qualified prospect. Be sure to subtract vacations, days you were sick, holidays, and so forth.

Let's say, for example, that you were able to sell for 200 days during the year. During those days you can sell eight hours a day, but of course you do not. In fact, you are lucky to get in four to six hours a day, and that is fine if you are hustling. Now take that 200 days times 6 hours a day and you get 1,200 hours of actual selling time. Divide that by how much money you made last year. Let's say you made $50,000. Your selling time is worth $41.66 an hour. Not bad. (Of course, if you made more or less than that, your hourly selling time needs to be adjusted accordingly.)

You may find that the actual time you spend presenting to clients is only four hours a day. That is not unusual. If so, you can up your hourly amount to $62.49 an hour. Your annual selling income is a fixed amount for that period. Yet, the lower the number of hours you actually were on the phone selling to a client, the higher your hourly selling income is. For this exercise, it does not pay to cheat. We are not impressed with the total amount of time you put in, only with the amount of money you made compared with that time. The smaller the number of hours, the more impressive it is.

Let's go back to the original number of $41.66 an hour. At that rate, if you had just spent an extra 10 percent of your time selling—another 20 days a year or 120 hours a year—you would have made an extra $5,000. Your time is very valuable. At the larger number of $62.49 per hour, you would have made an extra $7,500.

Phone Log Sheets

A phone log sheet is one simple way to track your phone calls. A sample is included here. You obviously will want to adapt the log to suit your specific needs.

At the top of the log sheet you should have places for the week of your call, the date, and your name. The left vertical column of the log sheet should be marked off in one-hour segments from 8 A.M. to 8 P.M., with a total at the bottom.

Going horizontally across the top, you might want six different rows. The first one in our log sheet is entitled "prospect calls." It means that if you are making a cold call and you get to talk to someone, you would make a tally mark in that row next to the appropriate hour. The next heading is "prospect qualified." If, during that same call, you do qualify the lead, you would place a second tally mark in that box corresponding with the appropriate hour.

The third heading is "qualified callback." This is for a prospect who has been qualified, has been sent information, and whom you are now following up. The next two headings, "messages left" and "messages returned," are marked every time you leave or receive a message. You may want to experiment to see if you do get messages returned. In our operation, we get about 40 percent of the messages returned, even in a cold-call situation. The nice thing about a returned message is that you get to make the presentation, because the person you want to talk to has called you.

The last heading is "presentations delivered" and is really the most important. This gets a tally mark whenever you spend time on the phone presenting information that furthers the sales process along. Leaving a message with a secretary is not a presentation.

SECTION 6, EXERCISE 5

On the following telephone tracking sheet, color in the box with a black marker for the time periods that you think are your prime selling time. Then go back and place a large "X" through those days and time periods that are mediocre calling times.

	MON	TUE	WED	THU	FRI	SAT	SUN
8:00							
9:00							
10:00							
11:00							
12:00							
1:00							
2:00							
3:00							
4:00							
5:00							
6:00							
7:00							
8:00							

SECTION 6, HOMEWORK ASSIGNMENT 1

On the following page you'll find a telephone log sheet. Your homework assignment is to make 35 copies of this log sheet (this is the only part of the workbook you're legally allowed to copy) and use one sheet per day for the next month. Feel free to customize this sheet to best suit your needs. At the end of each week, prepare a summary sheet; also prepare one at the end of the month.

SECTION 6, HOMEWORK ASSIGNMENT 2

Go back once again to Exercise 2. See if any responses have three "X's" in front of them indicating it's both a high-payback idea and the person in charge is either you or someone you work very well with. Your assignment is to put that one idea into action tomorrow (or the next working day).

If you don't have a response with "XXX" in front of it, then choose any of the four responses with either "X" or "XX" in front of it. Choose the one you think is both a valuable use of the idea as well as reasonably simple and easy to implement. Do it tomorrow.

Figure 9-2 Tele-selling phone log sheet helps you track your calls.

So, it is possible to have up to three tally marks for any one phone call. Let's say, for example, that you make a call at 10:15 to a new prospect. You mark the sheet at 10 with a tally mark under the first heading of prospect calls. After your call, let's say that the prospect became a qualified lead. Make a tally mark in the second column at the 10 box. You would also make a third mark in the far right column for presentations delivered.

At the end of the day, total each column. Once a week or once a month, take another sheet and add it all up for that period of time. On a monthly basis, you can then see a pattern. For example, if you are making a lot of calls between 8 and 9 A.M., but a much smaller percentage of them are getting through to allow you to present, you may want to adjust your prime calling time to an hour later. By the same token, if you are making a good percentage of presentations in the last hour of the day, which is perhaps from 4 to 5 P.M., then you should test the 5 to 6 P.M. hour to see how good it is for you. Moreover, if you are calling throughout the country, you have to take into account the different time zones.

We find, for example, that because we are calling on businesses, the more calls we make between 9 A.M. and noon, the better the entire day goes. This is because we leave a lot of messages in the morning that often get returned in the afternoon.

The summary of information you gather from these tracking sheets tells you, first of all, how many calls you are making in a day. Thus, you may wish to figure out ways to make more calls in that same amount of time. You can also discover how many calls you have to make before you get to make a presentation and how many presentations you must make before you get a sale. You can also find the relationship between messages left and those received.

Now you can take that information one step further and determine how these various activities affect your actual sales and earned commissions. As you can see, the top half of the chart is a summary of telephone activity over a three-month period. The second part is information you have at hand but not on the tracking sheets: total number of sales, sales of specific products or services, total dollars sold, and so forth.

The bottom half of the chart is for calculations based on all this information, including your average number of calls per working day, the dollars you have earned per call or per presentation, and how many calls or presentations you had to make to get a sale.

RMT TELEPHONE DAILY LOG SHEET
Confidential—Do not remove from office

Date _10-2_ Salesperson _MB_ Week of _10-2_ Total Dials _62_

	Cold Call	Qualified Call Back	New Lead Qualified	Message Left	Message Returnd	DisQual'd or Killed	Tickler File	Presentations Delivered
8:00								
9:00								
10:00	JHT JHT //		//	///				HHT
11:00	////	HHT HHT	//	HHT /	///	/	/	///
12:00	HHT	///	/					
1:00								
2:00	////	HHT //		////		/		///
3:00	////	////		///	///	/		/
4:00	HHT ///	//		HHT	//			/
5:00								
6:00								
7:00								
Total	37	26	5	21	8	4	1	13

New Qualified Leads

- EASTMAN KODAK
- DUNLOP TIRE
- AAMCO
- CA HOTEL/MOTEL
- ATLANTIC ASSN.

Notes:

Call Back Progress

	2nd In Ex CP Dead
	2nd In Ex CP Dead
	2nd In Ex CP Dead
	2nd In Ex CP Dead
	2nd In Ex CP Dead

Figure 9-3 Sample tracking sheet tells you a great deal about your calling habits.

At the very bottom is a sensitivity chart that projects what your sales and commissions would have been had you made between 5 and 30 percent more calls. It is a real eye-opener.

Tracking information is very helpful to you if you wish to become a better salesperson. We are always looking for ways and gadgets that can help us do just that. According to an article that appeared in *Direct Marketing* magazine,

> it is wise to work within a structure that will produce quantitative and qualitative data for the applications to be pursued. The first step in the process is to look for numbers that might be used as norms. The key in estimating telemarketing costs lies with two sets of numbers: (1) cost per call for handling inbound calls from business firms and consumers; and (2) cost per call per decision-maker contact in making outbound calls to business firms and consumers. Worksheets can be developed for inbound and outbound costs. The process also involves: (1) using the sales call ratio advantage or telemarketing as a base to compare sales cost; (2) determining the present cost of acquiring new customers; (3) looking at the first-year results; (4) exploring the time compression potential as it relates to acquiring 1,000 new customers; and (5) determining the chances for success.[1]

Phone-Calling Tracking Machine

Although this article suggests a good place to start, we feel your data gathering and analysis should go much further. The first step is to gather the information. If you do not want to take the time to do the tally sheets, consider having your calls tracked automatically. This can be done with a device from Radio Shack called a telephone accountant. It looks like a calculator without the number pad and hooks directly into the telephone line. It prints on calculator tape the date, time, and length of each call. It distinguishes between incoming and outgoing calls. For incoming calls, it tracks how many times the phone rang before it was answered. For outgoing calls, it records the phone number called and allows you to put up to 100 different two-digit codes after each call, so you can track the type of call you made.

---

[1]Bob Stone and John Wyman, "The Mathematics of Telemarketing," *Direct Marketing* 49, no. 8 (December 1986): 46–52.

```
            XX
11-02-89  08•06
#16173673600
    =0•01•27

            XX
11-02-89  08•13
#17037392782
    =0•01•086

            XX
11-02-89  08•15
#16158594522
    =0•01•54

            XX
11-02-89  08•17
#12168426000
    =0•01•11

            XX
11-02-89  08•19
#12146308787
    =0•00•59

            XX
11-02-89  08•20
#13015277701
    =0•01•31

            XX
11-02-89  08•22
#15137614371
    =0•01•54

            XX
11-02-89  08•25
#16154445533
    =0•00•10

            XX
11-02-89  08•34
#171683668101
0
        =0•01•21

            M1
11-02-89  08•48
    =#+    000
    =#+%000
    =#×    000
    =#×*  015
```

Figure 9–4. Telephone accountant printout.

Although this device was designed for people who need to track the length of each call so they can charge a specific account, it is perfect for recording much of the same information you get from your log sheet. It also automatically prints out a summary of calls at midnight or on request. We have used this device and it does a good job of tracking but, unfortunately, our experience has been that it tends to break down.

The coding feature is interesting. Before you hang up, you simply push any two digits on your phone and those numbers show up on that call as a special code. In our office, we assign everyone a range of numbers, like 10, 20, 30, and so forth. Each person has 10 different codes to use. In Jeff's case, he is 50, which means his codes are 50 through 59: 50 is a cold call, 51 is a qualified cold call, 52 is qualified call back, and so forth. So, not only does he know who made the call, but also the reason for the call.

If you make calls on a number of lines, you need one device per line. There are more elaborate computerized systems that can service an entire phone system, but they cost thousands of dollars. Ask your telephone vendor for more information.

Lead Cards

We also recommend that instead of calling leads from a book, you work from lead cards. A lead card contains the key information about the client: name, title, address, phone number, time zone, secretary or filter's name, and a place to track each phone call you make. We use an 8½-by-11-inch card. The cards are printed in four different colors to show which time zone the lead is in. This is important when calling all over the country. There is a three-hour time difference between Columbus, Ohio, and Los Angeles, so we cannot even begin to call the West Coast till 11:00 A.M. our time. Having the color-coded cards makes it easier to plan your day. If time zones are important to your sales, and you do use color coding, be sure to use four light colors so you can easily read what you have written. Colors we use from our quick printer are white, yellow, ivory, and light blue.

If security is a major concern, have your lead cards printed on a bold red stock. It will not photocopy well at all. Your other option

STREET SMART TELE-SELLING LEAD CARD

Confidential. Do Not Remove From Office.   AE _____ Date _____ Status _____

Company _____   Phone _____ Ext ____

Contact _____   Title _____

Address _____   Sec/Assist _____

City _____ State _____ Zip_____   Fax # _____

Description _____   Source _____

Date	Summary of call	Recall Date
__/__	_____	__/__
__/__	_____	__/__
__/__	_____	__/__
__/__	_____	__/__
__/__	_____	__/__
__/__	_____	__/__
__/__	_____	__/__
__/__	_____	__/__
__/__	_____	__/__
__/__	_____	__/__
__/__	_____	__/__
__/__	_____	__/__
__/__	_____	__/__
__/__	_____	__/__
__/__	_____	__/__
__/__	_____	__/__
__/__	_____	__/__
__/__	_____	__/__
__/__	_____	__/__
__/__	_____	__/__

Figure 9-5   Tele-selling lead card.

is to make sure you use a very light blue felt tip pen or pencil. It, too, will not reproduce well.

Also, the survey questions we use to qualify prospects are on a sheet of paper in front of us with spaces between the questions, so we can make notes right on the sheet. We use one sheet per prospect.

You can even merge the prospect lead card with your survey sheet so it is all in front of you for your call. You have the notes right there for your callbacks. Doing this ahead of time saves you much prime calling time.

Wall Charts Displaying Qualified Lead Status

It often helps to see where you are by having a wall display that allows you to categorize your leads according to status. We use the following categories:

- qualified lead,
- second contact,
- interested,
- excited,
- contract pending,
- sold, and
- dead.

Of course, you will want to change these categories to best suit your particular needs and setup. The challenge is to be able to move the card with the appropriate information to the proper category. Just writing the prospect's name on an erasable chart does not work because, as soon as that prospect's status changes, either up or down, it becomes more difficult to keep your system up to date. Therefore, you need a system in which each lead is placed on its own card. It sounds easy, but we experimented with a number of different systems until we found a few that would work well.

Besides changing the status column easily, you can gain insight into your progress by color coding the cards by month. In the system that we use, five colors are available:

- white,
- blue,
- yellow,
- red, and
- green.

We use the different colors to represent months. In the listing above, it might work like this:

- white = January
- blue = February
- yellow = March
- red = April
- green = May

Then they start to repeat again. By color coding the month, when you start putting up your qualified leads on your status board, you can see at a glance not only how many leads you have for a given month, but how fast they are progressing through the system. In our organization, we use a 90-day test for "decision mode." If the prospects cannot make a decision in 90 days, we put them in a tickler file until they can. By the same token, if a given lead does not change status within a reasonable amount of time, we need to be aware of it. So, if we are looking at the status board in April and still see white or blue cards in the first two columns, we know these leads are not moving fast enough. The idea is to move numerous quality leads through the sales system.

You can choose from a few systems in implementing this process. They are:

The Lynx Filing System

This gray plastic modular wall planner of "T" cards makes a good status board for tele-selling. At a glance you can see the status of store managers and their Streetfighting marketing efforts. You can customize it to suit your specific needs by the size of the cards and the number of rows of cards. Prices can vary from $40 to $500 depending on what you need. Get the catalog to see how this might help you. This product is available through

Remarkable Products.[2] (See the "Streetfighter's Resource Guide" at the end of the book.)

Index Card Filing System

Similar to the Lynx, the Index Card Filing System from Caddylak Systems, which does the same thing, uses regular 3-by-5 index cards instead of T-Cards. Only the top one inch of each card remains visible at all times for quick reference. This filing system comes in 3 sizes:

25" x 19"	4 columns with 12 cards/column	$ 99.95
37" x 25"	6 columns with 17 cards/column	$199.99
49" x 37"	8 columns with 27 cards/column	$329.95

The Index Card Filing System is more costly than the Lynx but is sturdier and more professional looking. The index cards are easier to deal with than the "T Cards" used by the Lynx. Here is a hint for getting more cards out of your system: Turn the cards from horizontal to vertical and you can create almost twice as many columns if you like. More information shows at the top, and you have only three inches across instead of five inches, but for most StreetSmart Tele-selling offices, it would work fine.

The Post-It Low-Cost Alternative

If your budget is tight, you can create a status board system by using 3M Post-It™ notes. Print out the pertinent information on a large Post-It and just stick it to the wall under the right category. Large Post-It notes are available in different colors so you can color code by month, if you wish. As certain prospects get upgraded or killed, they are easily moved. At a glance, you know how many leads you are dealing with, as well as the relative status of each one.

The TeleMAGIC Alternative

If having a wall chart or large display is not important, you can use a computerized telemarketing program such as TeleMAGIC, which is discussed in more detail later in this chapter. Provided

---

[2]The Lynx System is available through Remarkable Products, 245 Pegasus Avenue, Northvale, NJ 07647. 201/784-0900. FAX 201/767-7463.

you keep your contact files up to date, and if you have a field specifically for tracking status, you can create a filter that allows you to print out a report, as often as you like, of all the prospects in certain categories.

Speed Dialer

Many time-saving devices are available to help keep you selling more during your peak time. One device important to tele-sellers is an automatic speed dialer. This device can save you much time during the peak calling period, because it allows you during your off-peak selling time to program the numbers you will be calling at peak time. You can program the number when you are filling out your lead cards; then just mark the one-, two-, or three-digit code on the card. Because you are likely to be dialing that same number more than once, the automatic speed dialer will keep you from dialing wrong numbers. As a lead gets disqualified, you can fill a spot on the dialer with a new lead when you reprogram it in preparation for the next day's tele-selling.

Many phone systems have this feature built in. If yours does not, you can get a device that provides the same function at many electronics stores such as Radio Shack. Prices can range from $25 to more than $100. Get one that can hold at least 100 numbers, as well as speed dial. If you work from your desk, you will want a dialer that plugs into the phone. If you travel a lot, get a portable one that you can hold up to a phone.

Recording Your Sales Presentations

Telephone recording devices allow you to save and review your actual presentation. This helps you to improve your presentation techniques, voice clarity, voice inflection, objection handling, and other aspects of your StreetSmart Tele-Selling activities. There is nothing like hearing yourself, after the fact, to open your eyes to more effective selling. Telephone recording devices are available that plug into your phone or the phone line. Some also work with a standard cassette recorder that contains both a microphone plug and a remote plug. Once you set your recorder, the telephone device comes on only when you lift your handset, and it stops when you hang up. It is automatic, and you can forget that you have it working. Be sure to use a recording device with a built-in counter that allows you to return to a specific point on a tape. For example, if there is a certain phone call you want to review later, in off-peak selling time, you can jot down the counter number while you are talking, then rewind the tape and find the conversation later.

Keeping Your Hands Free

Headsets

When you must spend a great deal of time on the phone, it is best to keep your hands free while you talk, listen, and take notes. To do this, consider getting a high-quality telephone headset. A headset saves wear and tear on your neck, but make sure you get a good one. Headsets are sold in models that are cordless or with a cord. The cordless headsets sound a little hollow, so it is better to use the corded one, which costs in the $100 to $150 range. A company called Plantronics[3] offers several different models that are excellent. (See the "Streetfighter's Resource Guide" at the end of this book for more information.)

Long Cord

Whether you use a handset or a headset, however, you should consider getting a 25-foot-long coiled phone cord. The long cord enables you to move more freely about your office. Each of our phones has one. The long cords are inexpensive, and you can get them at any telephone store.

We do not like using speaker phones. Even the good ones make your voice sound hollow. We sometimes use them after we have built up a rapport with a client. If we are working on projects where we have to take notes, we sometimes will ask a client: "Can I put you on my speaker so I can take some notes?" That is really the only time we do it, because of the poorer sound quality.

Incidentally, here is a creative way of using a speaker phone. When you just cannot seem to get past the gatekeeper, you might

---

[3]Plantronics, 345 Encinal Street, Santa Cruz, CA 95060-2132, 800/538-0748, 800/ 662-3902 in CA.

try calling one more time on the speaker. When the secretary comes on, ask to be put through to the prospect. Then mention that it would help to put him on quickly while you are still in range. Now you have not said anything about a car phone, but that is what the secretary may think, and for some reason, there is usually a sense of urgency associated with a car phone. You may be put through. Keep this important point in mind, however. It is fine to be creative, and it is okay to leave out a few bits of information so the gatekeeper can come up with his or her own impressions. But please be careful not to lie to anyone. It is not a good practice, and it is not good business. You might even want to think twice about using some of these fringe techniques we have suggested.

Cellular Phone

If you spend much time in your car, especially if your particular product or service requires that you are out in the field calling on clients, then a cellular phone is a must. The cost of cellular phones has come down and the quality has gone up rapidly. Time in your car is dead time unless you can figure some ways to take advantage of it. A cellular phone is one way to turn that wasted time into productive time. A phone in your car is especially good for returning calls to customers, confirming appointments, and keeping in touch with the office. It could be great for cold calling, as well.

More on the Move

Other things you can do to covert wasted time to productive time in your car is to listen to motivational and instructive audio cassettes. You can also work on correspondence if you have a decent dictation recorder. On airplanes, if you are not doing the flying, you can use the time to get caught up on your reading and paperwork.

How Your Phone Personality Affects Your Sales

Items such as a long cord make it easier for you to move around, and that may also change your phone personality. With the freedom to move around, it becomes easier to convey enthusiasm about your product or services. Even though the prospect relies only on hearing you to get an idea of what you are offering, your excitement, or lack of it, is reflected in your voice and carried over the phone to your prospect.

Use facial and arm gestures as you would in person when making a point. When we are in the middle of an important presentation we like to stand and pace about to help keep the excitement going. It is also good to smile while on the phone. Your prospect can "hear" when you are smiling and when you are not. For that reason, George Walther recommends you put a mirror on your desk, so you can remind yourself to smile. You can even put up a sign that reminds you to smile.

If you ever get the opportunity to go inside a radio station and watch the announcers work, the experience can be a real eye opener. Even though no one can see them, the announcers use a lot of body motions and gestures and even props to get across their point. They work not only with their words but with their tone of voice and inflection. One of our salespeople finds that he gets a lot of mileage when talking to potential clients because his pleasant nature comes through in his voice. He comes across like a very nice person that people just want to believe and help. He has also had a great deal of theatrical experience, both on and behind the stage, and he uses that experience in his tele-selling. Your voice is a very powerful tool and is capable of doing a great deal to help you, if you try to use it.

Dorothy Leeds, author of *Power Speak*, suggests that you keep your voice interesting through articulation, diction, and pronunciation. Dorothy, who is one of the country's leading experts on public speaking techniques, recommends practicing with your voice to create interest. In her seminar, she has participants read from Dr. Seuss's *Green Eggs and Ham* with varied voice quality to demonstrate how you can make your voice create interest just as much as the proper words can.

Articulation refers to using those parts of your body that control how you sound: your tongue, throat, jaw, lips, upper gums, and hard and soft palate.

Diction is how well you put all the sounds together. Good diction is important not only to being understood, but in how you will be perceived.

Pronunciation is how you deliver the words. This can vary from region to region. In some parts of the United States, people place emphasis on certain words in a different manner than people do in other parts of the country.

Pacing is another aspect of speech. The speed at which you deliver your message makes an impression on your prospect. It is often suggested that you should try to match the pace of your prospect's speech to make sure not only that you are understood but that you are not tuned out. Someone from Little Rock calling a prospect in New York City could drive that prospect up the wall if his or her pace is too slow. On the other hand, if the roles were reversed, a New York City sales representative calling a prospect in Little Rock might find it difficult to build rapport and trust. If the salesperson's pace were slowed to match that of the Southern prospect, it might help.

You can also use pacing to create more interest. Slow down for certain key phrases or words to draw more attention to them. By varying your pace, especially when trying to create excitement about your product or service, you can convey much more than just the words you speak.

Volume is another element to consider. You should also try to match the volume of your prospect or perhaps be just a little louder. Much depends on the quality of the phone line during your call. When you soften your voice for key words and phrases, the process also creates interest and excitement just as with pacing.

You may find that if you speak with an accent or if you speak to a prospect who has an accent, you will have to adjust your pace to make sure you are understood.

Computerize to Increase Your Efficiency

You should seriously consider getting a personal computer if you do not have one already. You can now get a very powerful machine for not a lot of money, especially when you consider what a personal computer can do for your sales career. According to an article in *Sales & Marketing Management,* computers can improve sales by up to 30 percent by providing central databases containing customer information. Several sales functions can be improved with the use of a computerized marketing information system. In addition to computerized telemarketing, these include: sales forecasting to help form trend and economic analyses, sample and quote tracking, inquiry handling, sales force management, competitive tracking, and marketing research.[4]

You may not need or want your computer to provide all of these functions, but the computerization of your telemarketing efforts in itself makes the modest investment in a computer well worth it. According to an article in *Direct Marketing* magazine, computerized telemarketing can increase sales productivity, reduce costs, improve overall sales performance, increase customer service, and enhance the capability for program analysis. Despite such advantages, many telemarketing centers are still completely manual. Yet computerized telemarketing can allow marketers to make exhaustive analyses of their customer bases to determine the accounts that would be best served by field sales representatives and those that would be better handled by telephone personnel. New business formations and business move-ins can be added to a prospect database with ease. Computerized telemarketing systems can automatically dial phone numbers, access online databases, and guide the telephone sales representative through a presentation. Such systems can also generate valuable reports on operator performance and call data.[5]

When we converted our office over from our old computers to new personal computers, we were surprised at just how affordable they were, considering that the new machines had 10 times the power and speed and 5 times the storage of our old ones. The desktop machine we use has a 40-megabyte hard drive. We put both a 5.25-inch floppy drive and a 3.25-inch floppy drive in the machine so we could use diskettes in both formats. This choice was important because we also have laptop computers that use the 3.25-inch floppies. Our new pc also has 1 megabyte of RAM, uses the 80,286 chip and runs at 12 Mhz. This means that it is pretty fast and has enough storage to handle all our needs. We are by no means computer mavens, so we give you this information from a

[4]John B. Kennedy, "The Computer in Sales & Marketing—Want Higher Sales Productivity? Start with a Data Base" *Sales & Marketing Management* 133, no. 8 (December 3, 1984): 66, 68.
[5]Richard L. Bencin, "Detailing the Benefits of Computerized Telemarketing," *Direct Marketing* 49, no. 2 (June 1988): 60–61.

lay person's point of view. The minute someone starts talking to us about bits, bytes, and bauds, we are lost. We just want to be able to turn the machine on and, after a little training on a particular piece of software, be up and running.

When considering buying a computer, you must take into account all the programs you plan to use on it. In our case, there are three primary programs. The first is a piece of telemarketing software called TeleMAGIC, which we describe later. The second is WordPerfect, which is our word processing program. We do a great deal of writing, including books and articles, and use this program extensively. Our bookkeeping and accounting are also done on the computer, and we had to take our future needs into consideration as well, when making our hardware and software choices.

The irony of this is that this computer, with all of its capabilities, cost just $1,750 complete with a monochrome screen and keyboard. Just seven years earlier, we paid $4,500 for a computer with only 64K of RAM and a 5-megabyte external hard drive. By the time you read this book, no doubt you will be able to buy even more computer for less money.

To ensure good service, we found a reputable company in town that not only offered great prices but also offered immediate turnaround when there is a problem. We simply bring the machine in and they replace the board or element that needs to be fixed and then send it for replacement. We are never without the machine for more than a day. They also make sure our software is loaded properly so all we have to do is bring the machines to the office, plug them in, and we are up and running. This kind of service is critical, so be sure to shop accordingly. Price is not your only concern when buying computer equipment and software.

A laptop computer can provide some of the same functions as a desktop computer, but, because it fits into a briefcase, you can take the laptop with you. When dealing with clients in the field, a laptop is a wonderful tool. In our case, we travel a great deal and have to crank out articles and manuscripts. Those long hours on airplanes and in airports and hotels are much more productive when we can do word processing on the laptop.

Laptop computers come with battery attachments so you can work for a few hours when power is not otherwise available. According to Kurt Brouwer, a West Coast investment adviser who was interviewed by *Ambassador Magazine*, "wherever there is a telephone, I have an office."[6]

The laptop that we use has the regular 8088 chip which is slower than the 80286. (At this writing the fastest chip was the 80486 but for our purposes, the additional speed in the chip, against the increased cost was not really worth it to us.) We do not really do that much computing as such, so the speed of the chip is not that important to us. Yet, if you expect to do a great deal of calculations and projections, you may want to consider a 286 or the even faster 386 or 486 machines. A built-in or external modem will be necessary when using a program that automatically dials the leads for you.

Another advantage of a laptop computer is that it allows you to take your entire client file cabinet home with you. This means that you can type the leads of the cold calls you will make the next day right into the computer. You need only put in the company name, contact name if you have it, and phone number. The address and other information can wait until after you have qualified them.

By doing this, you have improved on the idea of programming your leads into a speed dialer, because any telemarketing software worth its salt will dial the numbers for you. At first this may seem like a lot of extra work to avoid dialing the phone, but it does provide many benefits to you. First of all, it is very likely that you will dial that number many times before you finally get through to present, so you will not only save time on the first call but on all the other ones you will make before you qualify or kill the lead. Second, even if you disqualify the lead now, you can keep the lead in your database and mark it with a recall date for six to nine months down the road. People get transferred or fired, circumstances change, companies get acquired or merged. Also, if you work with other sales people, consider "trading" your killed leads. Sometimes, a different person with a different approach can move forward where another person cannot. It works to everyone's advantage, and by trading, you need wait only two to three months to work a "dead" lead.

So what kind of software allows you to do this? The one we use in our office is called TeleMAGIC. It is sold by a group called

---

[6]Chris Barnett, "You Can Take It With You/Mobile Executive," *Ambassador Magazine* (September 1989): 30.

Remote Control in Del Mar, California. (See "Streetfighter's Resource Guide" for address and phone.)

This program is designed for a single user or for users in a network, and it does everything you would ever need to do to be an effective seller by telephone. Anyone can use it without consulting the manual by using the help functions. Even a sales rep who did not know how to type and who had never used a computer before was able to pick it up in a very short time.

At its heart, TeleMAGIC is a basic database. The screen has two different ways of accessing a prospect, and you choose the ways. We like to use the company name as our primary ID and the last name of the prospect as the secondary ID. If a client calls in or you need information about a certain company, you need only enter the first few letters of either the primary ID or secondary ID and it appears on the screen.

The program tracks basic information like addresses and several different telephone numbers. It records the first date you opened the file and the date of your last contact. You can also program it to remind you when to call again.

In addition, it automatically dials the phone for you. It provides a place on the screen to take notes of each conversation (and automatically enters the date and time of the notes).

The program times all calls, has a mailing list and labels function, offers a built-in word processor, and handles scripting or the questions you will ask, including how to deal with the objections you anticipate you will get. It does letters, invoices, inventory, and more.

With all the data that the program collects about your calling activities and the files in the database, you can have many reports to check your progress and efficiency. A "quickie" lists option in TeleMAGIC generates reports that offer the capability to select a group of records according to primary and secondary identification and recall date field keys. Each record has 20 fields. Basically, the program automates all the extra functions we have talked about, including follow-up cover letters and notes. And it holds up to a million records.

If you are working with a couple of different computers that are not networked, you will want to have the ability to combine your databases. TeleMAGIC makes it easy to add one database to another, but then you are left with duplicates. When you find yourself in that position, you may want to consider another piece of software called *King T-UT*, a TeleMAGIC utility program that is available through Business Systems Consultants. They offer two versions, *King T-UT Jr.* ($99) and *King T-UT Sr.* ($198). Both of these programs allow you to find and eliminate duplicate and near-duplicate contact records. The senior version also allows you to merge contact records from two databases in which the note pads and the user fields have different data. A similar software package called *Duplicate Delete Utility* is available through a company called MBS Software.

There is one other piece of software you will want to consider when using both a laptop and a desktop computer in the same office. It's called *Laplink*, and it allows you to transfer data directly from your laptop to the desktop without having to use diskettes.

Any way you look at it, the trend is to computerize. Even financial institutions, which have been under constant pressure to incorporate a sales culture into their operations, are looking at automating their telemarketing efforts. According to *Bank Systems & Equipment*, a trade journal for the banking industry, vendors say that automated telemarketing systems can increase sales by 5 percent to 35 percent and can streamline operations by generating reports for the bank and follow-up letters and forms for customers. Banks and thrifts are considering these systems for marketing credit cards, student loans, car loans, certificates of deposit, and just about any type of credit-related product. Central to these systems are auto dialers, which dial the telephone numbers automatically from presorted data files, sort out and post busy and unanswered calls, and pass on live contacts to the bank's telephone sales representatives. Many systems have predictive dialers that can automatically pace calls intelligently, based on the average length of sales calls and the availability of the sales representatives. The article goes on to say that automated telemarketing systems also reduce paperwork.[7]

The growing trend toward computerization shows how far telemarketing has come and what you may find yourself up against when you are out there selling. In the "Streetfighter's Resource Guide" in this book, you will find a list of other recommended

---

[7]Arlene Iovacchini, "Autodial Phone Systems Help Reps Focus on Sales," *Bank Systems & Equipment* 25, no. 12 (December 1988): 84–85.

books, audio cassettes and videotapes, as well as devices to help you further your telephone selling career. Remember, your education never ends.

Building Momentum to Build Your Sales

In successful tele-selling, the numbers you must cope with can be staggering. Even so, there is another aspect you also have to consider: in a word, momentum. When you look only at the numbers, you can easily see that you can impact your sales by properly applying this idea. Obviously, your specific situation may be different. Your dollars per hour might be more or less. The number of delegatable hours might be more or less. The cost of hiring a part-timer to properly delegate to might be more or less. Yet the principle will work for you to the degree that you properly implement it.

But the additional hidden benefit of "momentum" cannot be seen in the numbers. The more sales you get, the more referrals, the more confidence, the more renewals, the more exposure, the more recognition, and the more everything you get. Success builds on success, so by making this big stride in your sales, you are likely to see a geometrical improvement.

Your attitude changes as well. Once you are at this heightened level, you find that you do not desperately have to have each sale as you did once before just to survive. Because some of the negative pressure is off, you will find that your selling style is more relaxed. Your customers will sense this as well. Sure, you want the sale, but you also want to do what is right for the customer. You now have the option of walking away from a sale that you know is not right for the customer.

Our own personal experience in this area drives this point home. When we were first getting our company off the ground, we would take any kind of consulting assignment that came our way, just to survive. At one point, a large manufacture of sewing machines wanted to use our services to develop a Streetfighting program for its retail dealer network. Our proposal called for working with 20 retailers for 12 months to develop the program. They wanted the program, but approved only a five-month program for five retail stores because the investment in the program would be far less.

We knew we would have a tough road to go with the scaled-down version of our program, but we did our best. And we did a pretty good job under the circumstances. But the program still was far from where it needed to be to show a level of success that would allow us to work with the client for a long time. That was the end of the project. In the last month of the program, we had our major breakthroughs, yet, because the contract had ended, we did not get an opportunity to develop the program further. Had we had more retailers to work with, success might have come sooner. With only one-fourth of the retailers that we wanted, it took much longer to develop the techniques.

The bottom line was that we had a great shot with a national company that could have given us tons of work for years had we stuck to our guns and insisted that they give us enough time and retailers to do the job right. Had we had the confidence one gets from *not* needing the job for survival, we would have been more aggressive in negotiations. It would have allowed us to insist on the level of the project that was needed to show success.

Now, many years after that painful experience, we do not just take on any project that comes our way. Within reason, we work with clients to suit their budgets, yet if they do not give us enough resources to do the job right, we do not do it. As a result, we get more jobs, and the ones we get turn out to be successes. It is all in the momentum.

How to Delegate Basic Tasks to Increase Your Sales

If you have a secretary or an assistant to whom you can delegate certain tasks, doing so will help you build even more momentum. Your time may be worth more than $40 to $60 an hour when you are selling, but worth minimum wage when you are doing basic office tasks. Consider hiring someone to do those tasks so you can spend more time making money. Even if you pay a highly qualified assistant $10 an hour to do your preparatory work, such as digging up good leads to call, handling paperwork, programming a speed dialer, or even running some personal errands for you, you still come out further ahead.

STREETSMART TELE-SELLING SECRET #30

> To increase your selling time dramatically, and thus increase your sales, delegate tasks that can be done by others who cost you much less per hour than your selling time is worth.

One good exercise for you to do is to write on a piece of paper all the different tasks you accomplish, other than actual telephone sales presentations, during the course of the day. Some of these tasks may include making coffee, filling out order forms, dictating letters, compiling or processing client-requested information, answering non-sales-related phone calls, researching sales leads to call, and the like. Write them all down.

Next, go through each one of those tasks that you do and put a check mark by those that could be delegated to someone else. Then, next to the check-marked items, estimate how much time you spend on a weekly basis doing each of those tasks. Finally, add up all the time per week you spend on those tasks that could be delegated to someone else.

For the sake of argument, let's say you have at least 10 hours' work per week that you could delegate, thus allowing you to spend those 10 hours on selling. If your selling time is worth $42 an hour, and you potentially have 10 hours a week of selling time available to you, you could be earning an additional $420 per week! That is more than $21,000 extra per year. Now, take from that number what it would cost you to delegate it. Depending on the tasks, the labor cost could run you from $5 to $10 an hour, as already mentioned. Multiply those 10 hours by $10 per hour, and you have $100 per week in expense. Subtract that $100 from the $420 and you still net $320 a week or $16,000 a year more. (This example assumes 50 selling weeks a year.)

Taking a Quantum Leap with a Designated Cold Caller

After you have examined the nonselling tasks that can be delegated, you may want to consider delegating the most repetitious task of the selling process—cold calling. This is a big step, but if you are in a position to take it, it can really thrust you into new areas.

In the first chapter we talked about the various uses of tele-phone selling and how to conduct the initial qualifying and setup appointments. This use of tele-selling is particularly attractive if in your industry you need a special license to sell your product, such as insurance or real estate. There may be many people who would like to break into one of these fields but lack the legal credentials to do it. Such people can still work for you, finding you good, qualified leads and setting up appointments. While working with an insurance client in Florida, we noticed a growing acceptance of this approach. This particular company used CSRs (customer service representatives). The CSRs could not sell the products, but they could work as partners with licensed insurance salespersons to build the customer base.

The possible downside of having someone do your cold calling for you is that for each qualified lead you get, you have made one less personal contact than if you had made the cold call yourself. And when you think about it, you have actually made two less contacts because of your mail follow-up. Another down-side is that you are adding overhead to your operation. Yet, even if you work for a company that does not provide you with an assist-ant of any kind and your income is based solely on what you sell, you may wish to consider this approach, even if it means taking the initial money out of your own pocket to do it. If done right, having a designated cold caller could show you big returns.

If your designated cold caller works things right, he or she can actually set you up as an authority figure, so that by the time you actually meet your qualified prospects, either in person or on the phone, they should be a little in awe of you.

Using a designated cold caller is not suggested if you are just beginning your tele-selling career. On the other hand, with a year or more experience in your present field, you may be in a position to put on a designated cold caller at least on a part-time basis.

Compensating Your Designated Cold Caller

You will need to pay this person a base salary, draw, or hourly wage, plus a commission on his or her success rate. Instead of a bonus or commission on the qualified appointments set up, work it so that your cold caller gets a percentage of the business you close. That way, the cold caller's motivation is the same as yours—to work only the qualified leads.

Dr. Michael LeBoeuf explains this very clearly in his book, *GMP: The Greatest Management Principle In The World.*[8] The principle is, "The work that gets rewarded gets done." You want to make sure your compensation program rewards the proper behavior. In the case of a designated cold caller, that behavior is providing you with good qualified leads that are likely to turn into sales.

If you pay cold callers just by the hour, their motivation is to put in a lot of hours. If you pay them $10 for each qualified appointment, then you are likely to be working leads that may not be that great. They are being rewarded for the quantity, not the quality, of the appointments. On the other hand, let's say you pay them $25 for each appointment that they set up from which the customer buys something. Or you could pay them a percentage of the total sales. Now their motivation is in harmony with yours. They want you to work only the best leads because they make money only when you make money.

Emotional Support for Your Designated Cold Caller

Not only do you have to support this person with financial incentives but with emotional incentives, as well. It is critical that you have a great deal of personal experience cold calling in your industry before you take this step. Your personal experience enables you to prepare a system to support your cold caller. It is very difficult to set goals, objectives, parameters, and rules about calling if you have not personally experienced the process. This personal experience also gives you tremendous credibility with your cold caller when you offer suggestions and ideas on how to do the calling better.

After you have made cold calls for a time, you know what is realistic and what is not. For example, when we were doing our own cold calling in the beginning years of our business, both of us seemed to average about 50 to 60 dials per day. We also averaged about 12 presentations and two to three qualified leads per day. Of course, some days would be better and some worse, but this average was pretty reliable.

---

[8]Dr. Michael LeBoeuf, *GMP: The Greatest Management Principle In The World* (paperback, Berkley Publishing Group, 200 Madison Avenue, NY, NY 10016). Also available in six-cassette audio album through Nightingale Conant, 7300 Lehigh Road, Chicago, IL.

When we started bringing in cold callers, we had a good idea of what they should be able to do. Some constantly beat our numbers, but others were consistently below those numbers. After working with our first three or four cold callers, we found that our numbers may have been a little ambitious, so we adjusted them downward slightly. Still, we had a clear idea of what they should be doing.

Training Your Cold Caller

From our personal experience in cold calling, we were able to put in place a system that made it easy for a cold caller to get up and running. We already knew the qualifying questions, had all the forms and tracking systems in place, and knew what results we could expect, based on effort. After the callers acquired the basic product knowledge they needed to carry on semi-intelligent conversations about our products and services, we put them on the phone to start making cold calls.

Their first cold calls were to a special list. We chose small mom-and-pop retail stores in our area as targets for our Streetfighter's Profit Package, which is an audio and video training course that sells for just under $400. Of course, the main job of our cold callers is to call big companies and suggest our speaking and consulting services, but we did not want a green cold caller to contact a company that might potentially be worth tens of thousands of dollars in sales and make a mistake that would close that door forever. So, we used a list of small local retailers whom we normally never contacted anyway. This is how the new callers practiced. As it turned out, selling the $400 audio/video program to small retailers proved more difficult than selling a program costing 25 times as much to a large company.

We kept our cold callers on this program until they had some good sales. They would qualify the leads, and we would close the sales. In this way, we could judge just how effective they were at qualifying those stores, setting up the telephone appointment for a closer, sending out the follow-up information, and generally pre-selling the program. After a few weeks of this, we knew if they were ready to move up or move out.

STREETSMART TELE-SELLING SECRET #31

> The time to fire a designated cold caller is when the decision first crosses your mind.

We learned this valuable secret from Eugene Hameroff, Chairman Emeritus of Hameroff, Milenthal, Spence, Inc., a $30-million-dollar-plus advertising agency based in Ohio. Since Gene's retirement, he has been consulting for many small advertising agencies, and we became friends. His years of experience were a great help to us, but this one gem was priceless.

When you hire a cold caller (or any helper), you will know in your gut when things are not working out. You will probably find yourself wanting to postpone the inevitable, because firing someone is a painful experience for both of you—or at least that was what we thought. Once you reach the stage in your tele-selling career that you want to hire someone to do your cold calling for you, you will likely make a few recruiting mistakes. No matter how well this person interviews, you will not know how they are going to do until you get them on the phone cold calling.

Once you feel that a person is not working out, you have to let him or her go immediately. Any postponement hurts both of you. You may find yourself rationalizing why you should give them a few more weeks or even months. It will not help. If they are not doing it right now, they will probably only get worse.

This was a long, hard lesson, but now we can usually tell in the first two weeks if someone is going to work out. It took us a while to get to that point and you have to have some experience working with potential cold callers until you start to get a feel for it, too.

Recruiting the Cold Caller

We learned one recruiting method from George Walther, author of *Phone Power* as well as many other books, tapes, and videos, that has cut our cold-caller attrition rate dramatically. Interestingly enough, the bulk of the recruiting process is done over the phone! Here is how it works.

Run a small ad in the paper, usually on Sunday, advertising for a telemarketer. Just put the basics in the ad. People looking for jobs in sales and telemarketing tend to look at all the ads, not just the big ones. So save money by running a small ad with the basics. Besides Sunday, we run one on Thursday. These are the two days from which we have gotten the most response.

The ad that we run looks something like this:

CORPORATE SHOW BIZ

Fast-growing sales group needs experienced phone seller. Salary, commission, bonus, benefits. Unlimited potential. Call 000-0000 for detailed job description.

It doesn't take much more than that. People who are looking for telephone selling positions will call. Notice that we do not ask for resumés or give them a place to write. We do not want them to write. We want them to call. The number listed is at our office and is an isolated number hooked up to an answering machine. When they call, they get a five- to seven-minute outgoing announcement that describes the job completely. First of all, the introduction explains how the process works. It tells them they should listen to the announcement and feel free to call back and listen as many times as they like. They should also take notes if they wish. Then, based on what they have heard, if they feel there is a good match, they should call again and leave a detailed, audio resumé. Basically, they must sell us on why we should follow up.

The beauty of this system is that you get to hear how the person handles him- or herself on the phone. You do not care what they look like; you only want to know how they are going to come across on the phone. This process also saves you a lot of time interviewing persons who would not be interested enough anyway to succeed in tele-selling. We have found, for example, that a given ad may yield six messages, from which only three callers might be worth talking to. Yet, by using the Phone Accountant on that line for a couple of days, we know there may be 50 calls to that number. Think of the time you would spend answering 50 calls, mostly from people *wrong* for the job.

If you use this technique, further into the intro you can inform the caller that you will give complete details about compensation, but first you are going to give him or her a little background about your company and the products and services you offer. Get them excited about that; then tell them about how much they can make.

At the end of the tape, remind them once again how the process works. If they like what they have heard, they can call back and listen to the message again—as many times as they like. Encourage them to take notes and then to prepare an audio resumé response. Remind them that the purpose of the resume is not only to give you their past work history and accomplishments but to "sell" you on why you should call them back for another interview.

The next step is to conduct first interviews with the respondents you liked. You do this on the phone also. Once again, you want to hear how well they handle themselves on the phone.

If the telephone interview goes well, then it is time to bring them into your office for an in-person interview. By this time, you have agreed to meet only those candidates who have the greatest potential for you. The process has saved a great deal of your time and left you with only the best.

The following script is a condensed sample of the answering-machine outgoing message we use in our office for hiring telephone salespeople. At this point, we now hire full salespeople, not just cold callers. However, the same principles apply. You can use this message as a guide for developing your own outgoing message.

> If you are looking for a telephone sales position with unlimited potential, then you have called the right number. This is Jeff Slutsky, president of the Streetfighter's Retail Marketing Institute. In the next five minutes or so, I will explain to you in detail about this tremendous opportunity to make some great money selling by phone, but first I will give you a little background about our organization.
>
> We specialize in teaching businesses how to advertise and promote and generally increase their sales without spending a lot of money, which is a service that has become in increasing demand in recent years. You will find it interesting to note that we have gotten a great deal of national attention in such notable publications as *The Wall Street Journal, Inc.* magazine, *USA Today,* and *Success,* to name a few. Our client list is impressive and incudes AT&T, American Express, National Car Rental, Domino's Pizza, Ramada Inns, the City of Dallas, the State of Arkansas, and the country of India.
>
> We have been in business since 1980 and have had impressive growth during that time, and we have aggressive growth plans in the near future, as well—which is where you come in. We get our clients exclusively over the phone and have developed a very effective system and procedures for doing that. As a Streetfighting

telephone account executive, you will find yourself selling our services, which fall into three categories. The first service we offer is long-term program development and consulting programs. Second, we provide seminars, speeches, and workshops; and, finally, we sell a variety of products including our audio and videotape package. We also have a few books on the market. The first is entitled *Streetfighting: Low Cost Advertising and Promotions for Your Business,* which was originally published by Prentice-Hall, and our newest one, *Street-Smart Marketing.*

Now let's talk more specifically about the position. You will find yourself on the phone for the better part of the day. So you had better be sure that you enjoy telephone sales. This is not an entry-level position. Experience is important. Your compensation is a draw against commission. The draw is $0000.00 per month and the commission is paid at a rate from 10 percent to 20 percent, depending on the type of sale you make. In your first year, we would be disappointed if you didn't make $00,000, but it will require work on your part. If you put in the time and make the calls with consistent effort, if is certainly possible to hit those goals.

If this sounds interesting to you, I invite you to call us back at this number and listen to this recording again. Take some notes if you like. Then, when you are ready, leave a detailed audio resumé right here on the machine. We want to know your work history, your experience in sales—especially telephone sales—and why you think you would be good for this position. Sell us on the idea of calling you back and setting up an interview. Remember, this is your first sale, so think it through carefully.

Thank you for calling us and we hope to have an opportunity to work with you in the near future. Now here is the tone to start selling.

Put Your Compensation Program in Writing

STREETSMART TELE-SELLING SECRET #32

When hiring commissioned cold-call tele-sellers, protect yourself by putting your entire compensation program in writing, preferably in an employee contract prepared by your attorney.

When you start hiring people there is always the potential for disagreements over compensation. To do away with the possibility of a misunderstanding, have your compensation program in writing, with every contingency thought out in advance. To make this even stronger, you might consider having an employee contract or agreement drawn up by your attorney. Items to include are: how much the callers get paid and what the payment is based on; when and under what conditions they get paid; and what happens if they leave.

Designated Cold-Caller Strategy

As you start experimenting with your designated cold callers, you will, in time, begin to figure out what it is going to take to be successful at it. You will make mistakes. There is no way around it. You will have some turnover. There is usually no way around that, either. You want to find a person who not only can sell enough to set up good qualified appointments, but who has a personality that you can get along with and fits well within your office or business.

Once you start to get a feel for what works for you and you have a good designated cold caller on board, your next step is to hire a second one. Again, this is a big move, and you have to be careful. The reason that this move is important for you is that, as you become dependent on your designated cold caller, you also become at risk for losing that person. A cold caller may leave for any number of reasons,—there is always the possibility that your designated cold caller may leave you high and dry. When he or she is gone, your list of qualified leads and appointments dries up. You are then back in the position of having to do all your own cold calling, and that can slow your momentum.

The second designated cold caller is hired perhaps more for defensive reasons than for offensive reasons. Sure, theoretically you should be getting twice as many qualified appointments as before, but more importantly, you now have a backup in case one cold caller decides to leave you: Your leads will not automatically dry up.

With two designated cold callers, you have more liability. More overhead and supervision are needed, but you will find that there are some added benefits. Now you can create a little friendly competition between the two. Usually, one plus one makes two, but when it comes to competitive designated cold callers, you may find that one plus one equals three! Both work harder because of the competition.

The tendency we have found is for salespersons to jump a little too soon into using the second designated cold caller. Be careful. Remember that this is an advanced tele-selling move and should be started gradually.

Conclusion

STREETSMART TELE-SELLING SECRET #33

Your tele-selling education and training never end. The minute you become complacent is the time you start backsliding.

You should view your tele-selling career as a never-ending process. You will be constantly growing, evolving, and improving. At the same time, the marketplace will be changing rapidly. You will have to remain one step ahead, so make a commitment now to improve yourself—always. The many books, tapes, videos, seminars, and courses on a variety of subjects can help you do better. Take advantage of them.

This book is just a starting place. Developing and implementing a successful StreetSmart Tele-Selling program for your company or your own career requires hard work. There is no way around it. When you come right down to it, the biggest secret is that those who become successful tele-sellers work at it. They make an effort. They put in their time. They make calls. They are consistent about making their calls. They are not afraid to make mistakes, and they are willing to try out new techniques and ideas.

We have offered you many tips and pointers gleaned from experience. You must take the next step now and put these ideas to work for you. Every idea we present will not work for every kind of sale you may face. So modify, adapt, improve, and extract those elements that can make your tele-selling the successful adventure and career you desire.

Summary of the 33 StreetSmart Tele-Selling Secrets

STREETSMART TELE-SELLING SECRET #1

To get the best results from your selling efforts, choose the most effective tele-selling strategy. This strategy should be based on the appropriate combination of tele-selling phone calls and mail follow-ups for your particular product or service.

STREETSMART TELE-SELLING SECRET #2

In most selling situations, you can get a better return on your investment, in both money and time, if you use mail as follow-up *after* a tele-selling phone call, rather than as a softener *before* the phone call.

STREETSMART TELE-SELLING SECRET #3

Never try to sell your product or service to buffers or filters. Only sell them on putting you through to the decision maker.

STREETSMART TELE-SELLING SECRET #4

When you are being screened by a gatekeeper, follow up every question that you answer with a command statement to put you in touch with the prospect.

STREETSMART TELE-SELLING SECRET #5

Give the gatekeeper only the absolute minimum amount of information needed to answer his or her questions.

STREETSMART TELE-SELLING SECRET #6

Your initial telephone presentation opener, the first four sentences you speak, determines whether your prospect wants to listen to your presentation.

STREETSMART TELE-SELLING SECRET #7

Your first four sentences should consist of the following: (1) your introduction; (2) the benefits, solutions, or end results of using your products or services; (3) your new news; and (4) a negative question asking permission to make your presentation.

STREETSMART TELE-SELLING SECRET #8

If the name of your company telegraphs to your prospect your type of business, and if doing so might cause the wrong conclusion to be drawn about what benefits you really have to offer, use your company's initials in your opener.

STREETSMART TELE-SELLING SECRET #9

When making your first telephone presentation to your prospect, your first objective is to qualify that prospect to see if it is worth your while to pursue doing business with this person.

STREETSMART TELE-SELLING SECRET #10

To qualify your prospects properly, you must find out if they pass certain qualifying tests. Each of these tests depends on your business and the type of product or service you sell. Most, however, include some variation of the following: (1) want, (2) need, (3) decision maker, (4) decision made, (5) budget or credit.

STREETSMART TELE-SELLING SECRET #11

You should achieve four objectives in your initial phone call: (1) qualify your prospect, (2) set up an appointment for your next visit (either in person or over the phone), (3) get your prospect to agree to receive and review your mail follow-up, and (4) ask for referrals.

STREETSMART TELE-SELLING SECRET #12

Never allow your mailers to sell for you. They should only reinforce and help you build credibility and rapport with your prospect. All selling is done either in person or, preferably, over the phone, so you can personally guide your prospect through the buying process.

STREETSMART TELE-SELLING SECRET #13

The person asking the questions is in control of the conversation, and you have to be in control of the conversation before you can effectively guide your prospect to a closing point.

STREETSMART TELE-SELLING SECRET #14

Asking questions, not pitching features, is the way to uncover the real needs and problems of your prospect, which in turn allows you to offer your solutions and close the sale.

STREETSMART TELE-SELLING SECRET #15

Decision making is painful. When people are forced to make a decision, they feel pain and therefore use objections as a way to postpone the pain. A StreetSmart Tele-Seller helps the prospect to make decisions while keeping the pain to a minimum.

STREETSMART TELE-SELLING SECRET #16

Objections are good. They show that your prospect has interest enough to ask questions.

STREETSMART TELE-SELLING SECRET #17

To handle objections effectively, use the StreetSmart four-step approach: (1) soften, (2) isolate, (3) rephrase, and (4) suggest a solution.

STREETSMART TELE-SELLING SECRET #18

People do not buy products and services. Rather, they buy solutions to problems.

STREETSMART TELE-SELLING SECRET #19

Avoid painful words, such as "sign" or "contract," that put prospects on alert. Instead, use nonthreatening terminology, such as "let's give it the go-ahead, get the ball rolling," or "give it a try."

STREETSMART TELE-SELLING SECRET #20

In the minds of clients or customers, everything you say is suspect, but they believe that everything they say is the truth, whether it really is or not. Your objective in the selling process is to get prospects to figure out for themselves that your solution to their problems is the best one for them.

STREETSMART TELE-SELLING SECRET #21

You cannot debate affordability, but you *can* discuss cost and value.

STREETSMART TELE-SELLING SECRET #22

To close the sale, you have to ask for the order, and you often have to ask for it many times.

STREETSMART TELE-SELLING SECRET #23

Admitting a mistake and learning from that mistake is the key character trait of a successful tele-seller.

STREETSMART TELE-SELLING SECRET #24

The time to increase your sales is immediately after you have closed the deal. Have some post-closing, up-selling products or services that you can suggest just after the close that increase your sale by 10 to 30 percent.

STREETSMART TELE-SELLING SECRET #25

To close a sale on the phone, you have to have all of the necessary paperwork in the hands of the prospect, preferably in fill-in-the-blank form.

STREETSMART TELE-SELLING SECRET #26

It is easier to get repeat business and referral business than it is to get new customers, so use the phone to service your existing customers and keep them happy with you, your product, and your company.

STREETSMART TELE-SELLING SECRET #27

Providing service over the phone saves your customers time and money while involving them in your product or service.

STREETSMART TELE-SELLING SECRET #28

The only time you are making money is when you are on the phone selling. Use your primary calling time for selling and do all other tasks in nonprime selling time.

STREETSMART TELE-SELLING SECRET #29

Accurately tracking the results of your telephone selling activities helps you make improvements in all aspects of your tele-selling.

STREETSMART TELE-SELLING SECRET #30

To increase your selling time dramatically, and thus increase your sales, delegate tasks that can be done by others who cost you much less per hour than your selling time is worth.

STREETSMART TELE-SELLING SECRET #31

The time to fire a designated cold caller is when the decision first crosses your mind.

STREETSMART TELE-SELLING SECRET #32

When hiring commissioned cold-call tele-sellers, protect yourself by putting your entire compensation program in writing, preferably in an employee contract prepared by your attorney.

STREETSMART TELE-SELLING SECRET #33

Your tele-selling education and training never end. The minute you become complacent is the time you start backsliding.

Streetfighter's Resource Guide

Note: For your convenience, we have provided phone numbers as well as addresses of a number of useful resources. These addresses and phone numbers were current when this book was written, but please remember that addresses and phone numbers often change.

Books

The Great Brain Robbery by Murray Raphel and Ray Considine (Self-published. Murray Raphel Advertising, Gordon's Alley, Atlantic City, NJ 08401. 609/348-6646). Interesting stories and techniques for getting new customers. Fun to read and opens with some great examples of what we would call super "streetfighters."

Positioning: The Battle for the Mind by Jack Trout and Art Riese. To be successful, you need to know and take advantage of your unique niche in the marketplace. This book is must reading.

GMP: The Greatest Management Principle in the World by Dr. Michael LeBoeuf (paperback, Berkley Publishing Group, 200 Madison Ave., New York, NY 10016). Teaches you how to get other people to do what you want them to do, based on the following principle: The things that get rewarded get done.

How to Win Customers and Keep Them for Life by Dr. Michael LeBoeuf (Berkley Books, New York, NY 10016). The ultimate customer service book. Takes the concepts from *The Greatest Management Principle* and applies them to keeping your customers happy.

Working Smart by Dr. Michael LeBoeuf (Warner Books, New York, 1979). Time management and goal setting techniques. Also available in audio cassette.

The Unabashed Self-Promoters Guide by Jeffrey L. Lane (paperback, self-published). Ideas and techniques for promoting yourself. Helpful when you adapt it to selling yourself to your field management as a consultant and adviser.

Phone Power by George Walther. (Can be ordered directly from the author. 800/THE-TELE (800/843-8353). FAX 206/340-1160. 401 Second Avenue South, Suite 70, Seattle, WA 98104.) Shows you how to get the most out of your phone.

Power Speak by Dorothy Leeds (Prentice-Hall Press, New York. Can be ordered from the author: Organizational Technologies, Inc., 800 West End Ave., Suite 10A, New York, NY 10025. 212/864-2424.)

Smart Questions by Dorothy Leeds (McGraw Hill, New York. Can be ordered from the author: Organizational Technologies, Inc., 800 West End Ave., Suite 10A, New York, NY 10025. 212/864-2424.)

Successful Telephone Selling in the 80s by Martin D. Shafiroff and Robert L. Shook. Techniques for selling by telephone.

Perfect Sales Presentation by Robert L. Shook (Bantam Books, Inc. 1987.) Helps you learn sales from some of the nation's top sales people.

How to Close Any Sale by Joe Girard and Robert L. Shook (Warner Books, Inc., New York, 1989). Sales techniques.

Streetfighting: Low Cost Advertising/Promotions for Your Business by Jeff Slutsky. (Available directly from the author: Retail Marketing Institute, 34 West Whittier Street, Columbus, OH 43206. 614/443-5555.) This book was the predecessor to *StreetSmart Marketing*. You will find more anecdotes and examples of successful promotions, plus four complete chapters geared to getting the most from your radio, TV, outdoor, and print advertising.

The 33 Secrets of StreetSmart Tele-Selling Workbook by Jeff & Marc Slutsky. (Available directly from the author: Retail Marketing Institute, 34 West Whittier Street, Columbus, OH 43206. 614/443-5555.) Teaches you a Streetfighter's approach to telemarketing.

Audio Cassette Tapes and Albums

Note: We highly recommend the use of audio cassette albums whenever possible. From a time management standpoint, audio cassettes are the only medium for learning that can be used in almost any situation, including driving in your car, flying, and exercising.

The Greatest Management Principle in the World by Dr. Michael LeBoeuf. Teaches you how to get other people to do what you want them to do based on the principle: The things that get rewarded get done.

How To Win Customers and Keep Them for Life by Dr. Michael LeBoeuf, 6 cassette tapes (Nightingale-Conant Corp., 7300 North Lehigh Ave.,

Chicago, IL 60648. 800/323-5552.) Explains how customer service is critical for any business to be successful. Without it, your marketing efforts can only run you out of business faster.

Working Smarter by Dr. Michael LeBoeuf, 6 cassette tapes (Nightingale-Conant Corp., 7300 North Lehigh Ave., Chicago, IL 60648. 800/323-5552.) A good time management/goal-setting program for getting the most out of your time.

Phone Power by George Walther. (Nightingale-Conant Corp. Can be ordered directly from the author: 800/THE-TELE (800/843-8353). FAX 206/340-1160. 401 Second Ave. South, Suite 70, Seattle, WA 98104.) 13 individual cassettes that can be ordered separately at $12.95 each or as a "power pack" that gets you the videotape, free. The individual tapes cover different concepts, including phone power: (1) for the person who manages; (2) for effective communications; (3) for the receptionist; (4) for the switchboard operator; (5) for the secretary; (6) for the outbound telemarketer; (7) for the inbound telemarketer; (8) for negotiation; (9) for dealing with difficult people; (10) for the customer service professional; (11) for the salesperson; (12) for getting appointments; and (13) for the accounts Receivable collector.

Profitable Telemarketing: Total Training for Professional Excellence by George Walther, 6 cassette tapes (Nightingale-Conant Corp. Can be ordered directly from the author. 800/THE-TELE (800/843-8353). FAX 206/340-1160. 401 Second Avenue South, Suite 70, Seattle, WA 98104.)

Power Speak by Dorothy Leeds, 6 cassette tapes. (Can be ordered from the author: Organizational Technologies, Inc., 800 West End Ave., Suite 10A, New York, NY 10025, 212/864-2424.) Communication is always critical to helping you get your ideas across, and speaking to a larger group is important to your group training efforts. This book teaches you how to speak to large groups effectively.

Smart Questions by Dorothy Leeds. (Can be ordered from the author: Organizational Technologies, Inc., 800 West End Ave., Suite 10A, New York, NY 10025, 212/864-2424.)

Prime Prospects Unlimited (formerly called *Gold Calling*) by Bill Bishop. Self-Published. 8 audio cassettes. (Available directly from the author: Bill Bishop & Associates, 834 Gran Paseo Dr., Orlando, FL 32825. 407/281-1395.) This program is primarily for helping outside salespeople convert their door-to-door cold calling to setting up good, qualified appointments. Many of the ideas in this program were used for our tele-consulting techniques in Chapter 9.

Stalls Are for Horses, Not Sales People by Bill Bishop. Self-published. 2 audio cassettes. (Available directly from the author: Bill Bishop & Associates, 834 Gran Paseo Dr., Orlando, FL 32825. 407/281-1395.) Techniques for getting people to get off dead center and make a decision. Helpful in working with customers or store managers, when conducting field consulting.

Million Dollar Presentations (replaces the *Million Dollar Close* program by Bill Bishop. Available directly from the author. Bill Bishop & Associates, 834 Gran Paseo Dr., Orlando, FL 32825. 407/281-1395.) Some of the most effective sales and communications techniques found.

Managing a Retail Staff to Success by Harry Friedman (Self-published. Available from: The Friedman Group, 8636 Sepulveda Blvd., Suite C, Los Angeles, CA 90045. 800/351-8040.) Once you get customers in the front door, they have to buy or your advertising and marketing is wasted. This program helps you manage your sales staff.

Successful Retail Selling by Harry Friedman (Self-published. Available from: The Friedman Group, 8636 Sepulveda Blvd., Suite C, Los Angeles, CA 90045. 800/351-8040.) Techniques for getting customers to buy once they are already in your store.

Streetfighter's Neighborhood Sales Builders by Jeff Slutsky. 6 tapes/100-page workbook. (Available from: Retail Marketing Institute, 34 West Whittier St., Columbus, OH 43206. 614/443-5555.) Recorded live at a full-day seminar. Teaches you step by step the complete Streetfighting program. Comes with the *Streetfighter's Workbook*, which becomes your customized plan of attack.

StreetSmart Tele-Selling: The 33 Secrets by Jeff and Marc Slutsky. 3 tapes/ workbook. (Prentice-Hall, Englewood Cliffs, NJ. Available from the authors: 34 West Whittier St., Columbus, OH 43206. 614/443-5555.) Provides you a Streetfighter's approach to telephone selling techniques.

Video-Based Training Programs

Note: Video training programs are often the most effective way to convey information. They require more attention than an audio program, but they can provide you with the maximum amount of information in the shortest period of time.

How To Win Customers and Keep Them for Life by Dr. Michael LeBoeuf (Cally Curtis Co., Hollywood, CA, 1988. Can be ordered from the author: 504/833-8873.) Purchase price $575, rental $130.

The Greatest Management Principle in the World by Dr. Michael LeBoeuf (Coronet/MTI Film & Video, Deerfield, IL 800/621-2131). Three different programs are available, which teach you how to get other people to do what you want them to do based on the principle: The things that get rewarded get done.

Smart Questions by Dorothy Leeds (American Marketing Association. Can be ordered from the author: Organizational Technologies, Inc., 800 West End Ave., Suite 10A, New York, NY 10025, 212/864-2424.)

Phone Power Video by George Walther. (Nightingale-Conant Corp. Can be ordered directly from the author. 800/THE-TELE (800-843-8353) FAX 206/340-1160. 401 Second Ave. South, Suite 70, Seattle, WA 98104.) $54.95 or free when you order all 13 of his *Phone Power* audio cassettes. A great overview of George's entire "phone power" concept.

Prime Prospects Unlimited (formerly called *Gold Calling*) by Bill Bishop. Self-published. VHS tape. (Available directly from the author: Bill Bishop & Associates, 834 Gran Paseo Dr., Orlando, FL 32825. 407/281-1395.) This program is primarily for helping outside salespeople convert their door-to-door cold calling to setting up good, qualified appointments. Many of the ideas in this program were used for our tele-consulting techniques in Chapter 9.

Stalls Are for Horses, Not Sales People by Bill Bishop. Self published. VHS tape. (Available directly from the author: Bill Bishop & Associates, 834 Gran Paseo Dr., Orlando, FL 32825. 407/281-1395.) Techniques for getting people to get off dead center and make a decision. Helpful in working with customers or store managers when conducting field consulting.

Managing a Retail Staff to Success by Harry Friedman. Self-published. Available from the author. The Friedman Group, 8636 Sepulveda Boulevard, Suite C, Los Angeles, CA 90045. 800/351-8040.) Shows you how to teach your sales force to sell better.

Successful Retail Selling by Harry Friedman. (Available from the author: The Friedman Group, 8636 Sepulveda Blvd., Suite C, Los Angeles, CA 90045. 800/351-8040.) Teaches your sales force how to sell better.

Streetfighter's Profit Package by Jeff Slutsky. Package contains 1 VHS, the complete *Neighborhood Sales Builders* audio album with workbook, *Streetfighting: Low Cost Advertising/Promotion for Your Business,* and *Streetfighter's Advanced Training Manual.* Available from: RMI, 34 West Whittier Street, Columbus, OH 43206, 614/443-5555.)

Streetfighter's Tele-Selling by Jeff and Marc Slutsky, 1 VHS and workbook. See previous page for address. Provides you with a streetfighter's approach to telephone selling techniques.

Other Resources

Note: The resources suggested here may help you develop and implement your streetfighting program as effectively and efficiently as possible. In some cases we were provided samples to use and review, but we receive no payments, royalties, or commissions for these recommendations. These are suggested because we feel your program can be enhanced by their use.

Telemarketing: The Magazine of Business Telecommunications. (800/243-6002. One Technology Plaza, Norwalk, CT 06854-9977.) Annual subscription is $49 U.S. (12 issues). FAX orders: 203/853-2845.

TeleMAGIC Telemarketing Computer Software, written by Michael McCafferty. (Published by Remote Control Computer Support Group, 514 Via de la Valle, Suite 306, Solana Beach, CA 92075. 800/992-9952. 619/481-8577.) Computer software for single-user or multi-user telemarketing programs. Requires MS-DOS. Suggested machine requirements are 640K RAM, 20 megabyte hard drive, and a modem. Can work on machines with two diskette drives and 512K RAM.

Headsets of professional quality. These allow for hands-free telephone operations. Especially good for field marketing people who need to contact numerous neighborhood-level managers during the development and implementation phase of a neighborhood marketing program. Some retail operations using tele-selling techniques will also find headsets very helpful. Use professional-quality headsets only. Recommended vendor: Plantronics, 345 Encinal Street, Santa Cruz, CA 95060. 800/662-3902 (in California). 800/538-0748 (outside California).

Archer Telephone Recorder. Allows you to record your own telephone conversations. Plugs into any cassette recorder with a remote plug. Starts recording when you pick up the handset and stops when you hang up. Available at any Radio Shack store. Great for helping you review and improve your tele-consulting or tele-selling skills.

Duophone Computerized Phone Accountant. Tracks all incoming and outgoing calls on calculator tape. Tells you the length of each call and time and date and codes calls. If you are doing a lot of calling, this device can be very helpful. Not necessary if you use TeleMAGIC.

Good on only one line at a time (unless you get more units). Available at any Radio Shack. About $100.

King T-UT TeleMAGIC Utility Program. Item # 470000. (Business Systems Consultants, 2675 West Highway 89A, #401, Sedona, AZ, 86336. 602/282-9070.)

Laplink III (Available from Traveling Software, Inc., 18702 North Creek Parkway, Bothell, WA 98011. 800/662-2652. 206/483-8088.) Allows your laptop computer to share information with your desktop computer without diskettes.

The Lynx System status card holder is available through Remarkable Products. Comes with five colors of T cards. (245 Pegasus Ave. Northvale, NJ 07647. 201/784-0900. FAX 201/767-7463.) Catalog available.

Index Card Filing System. (Available through Caddylak Systems, Inc., 131 Heartland Blvd. P.O. Box W, Brentwood, NY 11717-0698. 800/523-8060. 516/254-2000. FAX orders 516/254-2018.) 30-day, money-back guarantee offered when item is returned in original carton. Catalog available.

Annual Planning Wall Calendar. Our favorite is the Smart Chart by John Lee Companies. (P.O. Box 398R, Crawfordsville, FL 32327. 904/926-7122.) They also provide some very helpful hints on using this calendar most effectively.

Index